Counselling and the Life Course

PROFESSIONAL SKILLS FOR COUNSELLORS

The *Professional Skills for Counsellors* series, edited by Colin Feltham, covers the practical, technical and professional skills and knowledge which trainee and practising counsellors need to improve their competence in key areas of therapeutic practice.

Titles in the series include:

Counselling and the Life Course

Léonie Sugarman

Los Angeles | London | New Delhi
Singapore | Washington DC

For
Dr Geoffrey Brown
– teacher, mentor and friend –
in celebration of his eightieth birthday,
and
Erica, Clare, Amy and Sam
– the 'Sugarman Peace' gang –
who, as fledgling adults, represent the future.

First published 2004

Reprinted 2014

SAGE Publications Ltd
1 Oliver's Yard
55 City Road
London EC1Y 1SP

SAGE Publications Inc.
2455 Teller Road
Thousand Oaks, California 91320

SAGE Publications India Pvt Ltd
B 1/I 1 Mohan Cooperative Industrial Area
Mathura Road
New Delhi 110 044

SAGE Publications Asia-Pacific Pte Ltd
3 Church Street
#10-04 Samsung Hub
Singapore 049483

British Library Cataloguing in Publication data

A catalogue record for this book is available
from the British Library

ISBN 978 0 7619 6239 7
ISBN 978 0 7619 6240 3 (pbk)

Library of Congress Control Number: 2003112202

Typeset by C&M Digitals (P) Ltd., Chennai, India
Printed and bound by CPI Group (UK) Ltd, Croydon, CR0 4YY
Printed on paper from sustainable resources

FSC
www.fsc.org
MIX
Paper from
responsible sources
FSC® C013604

Contents

'Activity Trail' Exercises

Acknowledgements

The present text has been influenced and much improved by the thoughtful comments and insights of generations of students at St Martin's College in Lancaster and Carlisle. In working towards their Diploma (Higher Education) in Counselling they have debated, engaged with, and challenged many of the ideas here presented. I am grateful to Colin Feltham for his editorial support, and wish that I could have done greater justice to all his suggestions for improvements and developments of the text. I would like to thank my husband, David Sugarman, for his support and encouragement; for providing a regular supply of tea, coffee and wine as I worked on the book; for ensuring that my computer and its software were always up to scratch; and for sorting out the sundry technical problems that beset the work at various, generally highly inconvenient, times.

Introduction

Assumptions about the existence of life stages and developmental sequences permeate our view of the world. Thus, the audience had a good sense of what was meant when Craig McDevitt (2000) spoke, in his opening remarks to the Sixth Annual Counselling Research Conference of the British Association for Counselling (as it then was), of the ability to do research being a significant 'mark of maturity', indicating how the profession was 'coming of age'. At the same conference Mel Ainscow (2000), talked of the professional doctorate in counselling as indicative of a 'maturing' profession; and Jane Speedy (2000) described different 'generations' of counsellor educators. Our understanding of such terms is frequently implicit and unexamined, and it is an aim of the present text to expose them to scrutiny and critique, and to consider their relevance for the professional counsellor.

Counselling and the Life Course introduces counsellors and trainee counsellors to the concept of the life course as a multidimensional and multidisciplinary framework for thinking about clients' lives within and, most particularly, beyond the counselling setting. For over two decades my interest in the idea of life span development and the concept of the life course has been sustained by the belief – reinforced through experience – that everyone has a story to tell. But we do more than tell our story, we live it. In large part, this book is about the importance of this story, and about different ways of conceptualising and telling it. It will be argued that both clients and counsellors can be seen as composing, in the form of a narrative punctuated by transitions and turning points, a life that is both unique and universal, using tools that are largely culturally determined. The book engages with the tension between, on the one hand, recognising age and life stage as rich, significant, but often overlooked, dimensions of difference and, on the other hand, resisting the invocation of frequently implicit age stereotypes and ageist discrimination.

My interest in this field has also been sustained by the belief that counselling can be a potent means of accessing and working with life

---

course issues so that, in the words of Studs Terkel (1975), what we live is 'a sort of life' rather than 'a sort of dying'. The impact of both counsellor and client age on the counselling relationship is considered, with different life stages being seen as characterised by distinctive vulnerabilities that are likely to find voice within the counselling relationship. At the same time, the concept of the life course is also used as an integrative framework for considering the commonalities between different life stages, thereby providing a focus for counsellors' consideration of how to draw on their extant skills and expertise when working with clients of a different age and life stage to that with which they are already familiar.

The present text has provided a welcome opportunity to write about the life course specifically for an audience of counsellors and trainee counsellors. My hope is that the concepts and models covered in this book will be both inherently interesting, and also provide useful additions to the theories and frameworks that currently guide your practice. An 'Activity Trail' of structured exercises is interspersed throughout the text in order to encourage reflection on the concepts discussed, and their significance for clients, for yourself, and/or for your counselling practice. My hope is that the book will be of relevance to counsellors irrespective of their particular theoretical stance. However, as most of my teaching is with students working within the person-centred approach, it may be that a bias towards this perspective can be discerned.

In this book I build on some of my previous publications in the field – notably a chapter in the *Handbook of Counselling Psychology* (Woolfe et al., 2003) and another, written jointly with Ray Woolfe, in the *Handbook of Counselling* (Palmer and McMahon, 1997). My book, *Life-span Development: Frameworks, Accounts and Strategies* (Sugarman, 2001) complements the present text by, for example, discussing the work of several theorists in greater detail, and also considering other topics, such as research methodology, that are not dealt with here at all.

Léonie Sugarman
May 2003

1

Composing a life

*'If you could see your life's shape, you would find its features to be, like
those on your face, universally human yet completely unique.'*

(Tristine Rainer, 1998)

Clients of all ages are constantly engaged in actively creating and
recreating their lives. They constantly adjust to changing circumstances and life events in ways that depend, at least in part, on their
biographical experience. In other words, life stage, or place in the life
course, matters to clients. It positions them in a social and family
context – perhaps as a part of the 'younger' or the 'older' generation;
or possibly within the 'sandwich' generation, caught between the
demands of teenage children and ageing parents. Models of the life
course can help counsellors orient themselves in relation to their
clients' lives, recognising how life problems take on a new hue in the
psychosocial contexts of successive life stages (Carlsen, 1988). The
present book strives to present the life course as a framework – an
aerial view, if you like – for conceptualising a range of ideas and tools
that are relevant to counselling at any life stage. These include things
like the experience of transitions, the balance between growth and
loss, and the tension between continuity and change. Even the most
assiduous of clients spend more time outside the counselling relationship than within it, and the concept of the life course provides a
framework for locating counselling practice within the client's wider
and evolving life space. When counselling from a life course perspective, clients are seen as 'existing at the centre of a matrix where life
events combine and conspire with the ageing process to present each

person, at any one time, with a unique set of challenges' (Woolfe, 2001: 347).

The life course

Counsellors need some way of encapsulating such human experience – a flexible framework that is both sufficiently substantive to anchor and support the disparate pieces that make up a person's life, and sufficiently malleable to accommodate the uniqueness of individually patterned lives (Gilmore, 1973). The *life course* (Runyan, 1978; Davey, 2001) – the rhythmic, fluctuating pattern of human life, marked out by sequences of key events and interactions between self and environment – provides such a framework. A life course perspective acknowledges that the trajectory from birth to death is highly personal and unique to each individual, and yet also contains experiences and events common to most members of a social group (Davey, 2001). It draws on material from individual, interpersonal, ecological and macrohistorical vantage points in order to understand human experience and behaviours (Silva and Leiderman, 1986). Within the life course, a person's *life span development* – the broad changes and continuities that constitute a person's identity and growth (Seifert et al., 2000) – can be explored.

Images will often communicate better than words the ramifications of a life course perspective, and these are the focus of Activity 1. This is the first stopping point in what can be described as an 'Activity Trail' threading its way through the text. The analogy is with the 'Fitness Trails' found in urban parks, in which city dwellers jog between 'posts' where they are directed to complete various specified exercises. Taken together, these activities are designed to address many of the key features of the life course perspective and, albeit to different degrees, engage all of Kolb's (1984) learning modes: active, reflective, abstract and concrete. My hope is that you will take time out from reading the text of this book to consider these activities as they occur, working either individually or with a group of peers. A comment on each activity is included in the Appendix. I realise it is unlikely that many readers will work systematically through all of the Activity Trail exercises – lack of time and/or motivation seems probable to preclude this. However, I do put in a plea for giving the activities some thought and, even if you have not completed them in their entirety, referring to the commentaries in the Appendix, which include relevant points and discussion not covered in the main text.

Activity 1: Metaphors of the life course

At its most profound, the meaning of human life is carried in metaphor. For few of us are the metaphors we live by explicit; we do not usually have any conscious awareness of living out anything beyond what seems to be our literal experience. Yet ultimately, it is the metaphorical sense we make of our living that gives the journey its direction, its sense of progression or development, its turning points, changes and passages, the meaning of its beginning and its end.

(Salmon, 1985)

Metaphors of the life course can express our meaning more creatively and subtly than formal definitions. Appealing to imagination as well as reason, metaphors can illustrate, illuminate and embellish our understanding. The concepts of the life course and of life span development are large and unwieldy, but metaphor can clarify this muddle. Consider the metaphors below, and, if you wish, generate your own. What does each say about the nature and meaning of the human life course? Expand them and extend their implications to find images most in keeping with your own world-view.

- Think first of visual images of the life course – a ladder, an arc, a circle, a tapestry, a tangle of wool. … What does each suggest about the nature of the life course? In what ways do they differ? Which resonate most, and which least, with your experience?
- Now extend the metaphor beyond a simple shape. Think about images from the natural world – a plant, a river, or a rainbow, perhaps. Think, too, about patterns of time in nature – a day or a year. What characteristics does each of these metaphors confer on the life course? To what extent are they adequate? What are their limitations?
- As a contrast, now imagine life as a game of cards. We are dealt a hand of cards at birth, and subsequently may receive, or take, others. Perhaps we will discard or lose some of our cards, and, depending on the rules of the 'game', we will have a greater or lesser say in how our hand is played. What does this metaphor imply about the nature of the life course?
- Another metaphor might be the life course as a musical composition – will it be a simple, traditional tune; a rap; a symphony; a jazz improvisation …? In what ways do each of these say something different about the life course?
- Finally, invoke the image of the story as a metaphor for life. What events will be included? What will be ignored? Will the story be dramatic and eventful? Will it mirror a traditional tale – a fairy story, perhaps? If so, which one? What does thinking about life as a story suggest about the nature of human existence?

An evolving life structure

The life course can usefully be thought of as an evolving *life structure* – a term introduced by Daniel Levinson and his colleagues to describe the sequential 'seasons' of adulthood (Levinson et al., 1978; Levinson, 1986, 1996). It is a non-hierarchical image in that, whilst seasons follow each other in a fixed order, none is inherently better or worse than any other. Each is an equally important part of the whole.

The life structure is an ecological construct – a composite of the person, their physical, social and cultural context, and the relationship between the person and the immediate world of which they are a part. For counsellors this is a useful framework because it allows attention to be focused, as appropriate on the individual, on external factors, or on relationships. Thus Schlossberg and her colleagues (1995) distinguish four factors that influence a person's ability to cope with change – self, situation, support and strategies.

- *Self*: what the person brings to the situation by virtue of who they are. This will include psychological attributes such as personality, values and level of maturity, and also personal and demographic factors such as socioeconomic status, gender, ethnicity, state of health, and – crucial in the present context – age or life stage.
- *Situation*: the particular characteristics of the circumstances in which clients find themselves. Significant factors will include the timing of the event, change or transition, what triggered it, the meaning of the event to the person experiencing it, and how much control they have over the situation.
- *Support*: the type and source of support available to help the person manage the change. Thus, the support may be emotional and/or practical, and may derive from intimate relationships, the family unit, networks of friends and colleagues, and the institutions and communities of which a person is a part.
- *Strategies*: what the person brings to the situation in terms of what they do – their coping skills and behaviours.

These different factors include both the person and the context in which the person is living. We are each a part of several immediate and interlocking settings – for example, home, workplace, school and, possibly, a counselling relationship. Each setting comprises a complex system of spoken and unspoken of demands, norms and expectations that both complement and contradict each other. Bronfenbrenner (1979, 1992) places these, and the relationships between them, in a still broader framework – a hierarchy of nested environments organised in terms of the directness of their impact on the individual. He distinguishes four levels within this hierarchy:

- the immediate settings of which the individual is a part;
- the network of settings and the interrelationships between them;
- the larger institutions of society – including education, health services and the mass media;
- the overarching values and patterns of the culture or subculture – including language, traditions and ideology.

Life structures include both the individual and the network of personal settings of which they are a part. Clarifying, managing and resolving conflicts between the demands of different settings is a frequent element in issues that clients bring to counselling. Societal institutions and cultural norms, in turn, impinge on these settings. The relationship is, however, two-way – with the individual influencing the environment as well as the environment influencing the individual.

Rather than being seen as a static framework, Bronfenbrenner's model is best thought of as a dynamic system in which the various elements vary in nature and significance across time and culture, and also in the course of an individual's life. Not only this, but people also change in ways that alter the meaning of the environment to them (Vgotsky, 1994). As we and our vantage point changes, environmental factors that had one meaning and played a certain role at a given age, may, over a period of time, begin to have a different meaning and to play a different role. This is what happens when parents renegotiate their relationship with their adolescent children as these children move towards adulthood. Young people who go away to college or university often experience the anomaly of having two places they call 'home'. They may feel disloyal and guilty when, in conversation with their parents during the vacation, they inadvertently refer to their university flat as home. In relation to when they were younger, the parental home now has a changed meaning and plays a different, although not necessarily irrelevant, role in their life.

Kahn and Antonucci's (1980; Antonucci, 1991) image of an interpersonal support convoy adds this element of change and development to Bronfenbrenner's model of overlapping ecological systems. An *interpersonal support convoy* consists of a network of relationships that surrounds each of us and moves with us through life, both providing continuity in the exchange of support, and changing in structure over time. It can be represented pictorially as a series of concentric circles, with the focal person at the centre, and with the most consistently important convoy members in the inner circle and with the most transient and role-dependent members on the periphery. This arrangement is considered further in Chapter 4, where Activity 10: Interpersonal support convoys, involves completing a convoy picture for yourself and for one of your clients. Interpersonal support convoys incorporate the concept of movement and change in that people enter and leave the convoy and, within it, a convoy member may move either towards or away from its centre as their relationship with the focal person waxes or wanes in importance. To communicate this visually, the concentric rings should, perhaps, be replaced by concentric pipes.

The life structure is not static, but evolves over the course of a lifetime through a series of alternating structure-changing (or transitional) and structure-building (or consolidating) phases (Levinson et al., 1978; Levinson, 1986, 1990). *Structure-changing* phases are periods of upheaval and decision making, typically lasting up to five years, and involve terminating one life structure and initiating another. By way of contrast, *structure-building* phases are periods of consolidation rather than upheaval, typically lasting five to seven years, and involve implementing and building on changes and decisions made during the transitional period. The alternating pattern of structure-changing and structure-building phases can be seen as giving a basic rhythm to the human life course – one that Levinson sees as universal across time and culture. Within this overriding rhythm, each phase, be it structure-building or structure-changing, has its own distinctive character and is distinguished by a set of characteristic (and often contradictory) tasks.

A particular implication of Levinson's theory for counselling practice is the recognition that clients' needs may vary according to whether they are in a transitional or consolidating phase. Exploration and decision making are likely to be the primary focus during structure-changing periods, with implementation of plans, maintenance of effort and evaluation of outcome becoming more important during the structure-building periods. This sequence mirrors to a considerable extent the sequence of stages in Prochaska et al.'s (1992) transtheoretical model of change: pre-contemplation, contemplation, preparation, implementation and maintenance.

The image of a life structure evolving through alternating structure-changing and structure-building phases helps to normalise the notion of 'seasonal' change during adulthood. It challenges people's often implicit assumption that adulthood is a plateau reached at the end of adolescence; an assumption that can lead to distress when disproved – 'If only I had made better decisions 5, 10, 15 years ago I would not be in this mess now'. The sequence also provides a framework for locating the study of particular life events or turning points, so that they are not seen as isolated states or experiences. 'The life course approach', wrote Haraven and Adams back in 1982, '... views life transitions and changes in work status and family relations as life processes, rather than an isolated state or segment of human experience. ... Rather than viewing any stage of life, such as childhood, youth and old age, or any age group in isolation, it is concerned with an understanding of the place of that stage in an entire life continuum' (p. xiii).

A 'seasonal' view of stages facilitates the valuing of each life stage for itself, rather than primarily a prelude to later, more 'advanced' levels of functioning. Such a position is consistent with Crompton's (1992) advocacy for 'childist' counselling, wherein counsellors work to enable troubled children 'to recognize and embrace their own reality, the inwardness which balances being and growth, stability and change' (p. 12). Crompton implicitly places childhood and the counselling of children in a life span perspective:

> A childist approach to counselling requires respect for the idea of childhood as well as for every individual child. If *feminism* involves the study of the feminine in all aspects of culture – for example, religion, politics, dress, art, literature, power, oppression – *childism* would involve equivalent study about childhood. ... A childist counsellor would begin with the idea of a child of whatever age being a complete person rather than an immature version of the adult s/he would become. *An acorn is not an immature oak tree; an acorn is perfectly an acorn. It contains everything necessary for growth into an oak tree but neither acorn nor tree contains greater or lesser value and virtue.* Each is entire unto itself, both are of use to other forms of life. (p. 5, emphasis added)

Life stage

Life stage determines, at least to some extent, the issues that we face and that we might bring to counselling. It also influences how we experience events that could occur at any age – the death of a parent will have many different implications depending on whether we are

2 years old, 15, 40 or 65. The meaning we give to our own and other people's behaviour is filtered through an awareness of age, expectations and norms:

> *At the age of 48 Maria was concerned about a range of things in her life that were 'not as they should be'. Her husband, two years her junior, had recently purchased a high-powered motor bike and was, in her words, 'trying to relive his youth'. Not only did she find this undignified and ridiculous, but she was also concerned that his biking skills were rusty after a quarter of a century behind the wheel of a car rather than the handlebars of a motor bike. As for herself, the traditional role of homemaker, to which she had always aspired, was more than beginning to pall – she not only wanted to spread her wings beyond the confines of the home, but felt also that not to do so would place her out of step with current expectations concerning women 'of her age'. She felt her options were reduced by the fact that her 25-year-old son had a history of mental illness and seemed unable to live independently, but she also recognised that this provided her with a reason (or was it more of an 'excuse' she sometimes asked herself) for not doing anything.*

A life course perspective provides a lens through which many aspects of the above vignette can be viewed. Maria is awash with assumptions, some of which she has articulated and others that may remain implicit, concerning what she and her family should (and should not) be doing at this point in time. She may be right that it is dangerous for her husband to be speeding round the country on a motor bike – skills can atrophy, and reaction times do slow as we move into midlife. But, on the other hand, perhaps experience will compensate for speed of response (or at least might have done if he had kept his biking skills up to scratch). The restlessness that Maria feels about her own role may reflect a natural outgrowing of a way of organising her life that, some 20 years ago, suited her almost perfectly. Also, it is not unreasonable for her to have expected, prior to her son's problems coming to light, that by this stage she would be free of the day-to-day responsibilities of parenting. She also has some awareness that times, as well as people, change – that whilst it may have been acceptable, and indeed, expected that women of her parents' generation would remain 'housewives' even once children were grown, now that is no longer the norm, and Maria feels compunction to widen her horizons.

Time and stories

The degree to which life span perspectives are taken into account in counselling and psychotherapy is extremely variable (Silva and Leiderman, 1986). Nonetheless, life stage, age norms and expectations form a backdrop to much of what clients bring to counselling. We cannot escape from the reality that lives are lived and understood in time.

> Imagine a past devoid of time information: a rich store of memories, some vivid, detailed, and steeped in affect, but all free-floating entities unattached to any time. This peculiar sort of memory would be like a jumbled box of snapshots, all clearly belonging to our past but resistant to any attempts at dating or sequencing. It is readily apparent that this is nothing like human memory for time; we have, instead, a clear sense that each snapshot belongs to a unique place in our past, that our life unfolds in time, that it is a chronology, a story, in fact a true autobiography. (Friedman, 1993: 44)

In this quote, Friedman (1993) invokes the metaphor of life as story that was a part of Activity 1 above. It is a part of this story that clients bring to counselling. 'Have you ever noticed', asks Howard (1991), 'that therapy usually begins with an invitation to the client to tell his or her story?':

> Therapists have favored ways of phrasing their readiness to hear the client's tale, such as 'Can you tell me what brings you here?' or 'How can I be of help to you?' or 'What seems to be the problem?' Clients generally know these invitations do not request the telling of one's complete life story. ... Rather, clients understand that their task is to tell the part of their life story that appears most relevant to their presenting problem. (Howard, 1991: 194)

Counselling and stories are intimately entwined. Counselling provides a place where client stories can be told and heard, discovered, created and reworked. The life course is the theatre where these stories are enacted.

However, counsellors can never know the whole of a client's life story. It is also probable that most counsellors will not in their day-to-day work see clients across the full range of the life course (although family therapists may be an exception to this generalisation). Most counsellors and many agencies focus on a particular section of the life course, and/or particular types of concern. Thus, whilst there are counselling texts that focus on counselling with clients at particular life stages, there are few with an explicitly life course perspective – Jacobs (1985, 1998), Thomas (1990) and Blocher (2000) being rare exceptions. Both the 1996 *Handbook of Counselling Psychology* (Woolfe and Dryden, 1996), and its 2003 second edition (Woolfe et al., 2003) included consecutive chapters on work with children and young people (Downey, 1996, 2003), young adults (Cooper, 1996, 2003), midlife clients (Brown and Smith, 1996; Biggs, 2003) and older adults (Twining, 1996; Goudie, 2003), but, again, this is fairly unusual.

A life course perspective provides a number of overarching 'meta-models' that enable counsellors to see clients' current concerns against a backdrop of the strands and rhythms that characterise the total life span. The particulars, in other words, are seen as elements in a larger whole. A life course perspective also provides frameworks to guide thinking and practice in relation to clients who might fall outside a counsellor's usual range of experience – providing conduits, as it were, through which knowledge and expertise can be funnelled into new arenas of work.

Activity 2: What is an adult?

> *As a boy, I was rather sickly, and my parents have told me that it was predicted I would die young. This prediction has been proved completely wrong in one sense, but completely true in another sense. I think it is correct that I will never live to be old. So now I agree with the prediction. I believe I will die young.*
>
> *(Rogers, 1980)*

The quotation above is taken from a chapter entitled 'Growing old; or older and growing?' in Carl Rogers' (1980) book, *A Way of Being*, published when he was in his late 70s. Rogers died in 1987, one month after his 85th birthday. Whether we consider him to have been old or young at his death, I imagine no one would dispute that he was an adult. Similarly, I imagine that the majority of people reading this book consider themselves to be adults. But what do we mean by this? If you are an adult, does that also mean that you are also grown up? To what extent are the two terms synonymous?

Either on your own or, preferably, with two or three others, try to formulate definitions of:

(1)   an adult, and
(2)   a grown-up.

Questions to prompt your reflections include:

- What does it mean to be an adult?
- How does an adult differ from a child?
- Can you be an adult without being grown up?
- Can you be grown up without being an adult?
- How do you know when you are grown up?
- How grown up are you?

Age

Activity 2 asks the question 'What is an adult?', and one of the con-
clusions generally reached by those completing it is that age occupies
an anomalous position in the life course. On the one hand, age is, to
a greater or lesser extent, an almost inevitable anchor point in
accounts of the life course, and an important prism that, along with
other attributes such as gender, class and ethnicity, filters how we
perceive and interact with each other. When we meet someone for
the first time – and this includes first meetings between counsellor
and client – one observation we make is with regard to that person's
age in relation to our own. The other person is 'a young man like
me', 'old enough to be my grandmother', 'the same age as my little
brother' etc. And we adjust our behaviour – our language, manners
and conversation – accordingly.

   On the other hand, we all know that age tells only part of the
story; and the part that it tells it may not tell clearly or accurately:
'I don't feel 50', we may say. 'You don't look 50', we may be told. But
what does '50' feel and look like? 'Fifty' feels like a 50-year-old feels.
'Fifty' looks like a 50-year-old looks. Feeling and looking 50 will be
very different for different people. And yet, it can be difficult to get a
clear picture of a person if we do not know their age. Age, somewhat
mercurially, can be both crucially important and totally irrelevant.

Ageism

Ageism – the systematic stereotyping of and discrimination against
people because of their age – is a complex issue that is itself not
immune from ageist thinking. Although it is most usually regarded
as being something that is directed at older people, it is
better thought of as prejudice based on age, not specifically old age
(Itzin, 1986; Johnson and Bytheway, 1993). As with other forms of

oppression, such as sexism and racism, it involves attributing characteristics to individuals simply by virtue of their membership of a particular group. As with other forms of oppression, it is reinforced by the structures of society, with age being used as a gatepost restricting access to services, privileges, entitlements and responsibilities. As a form of oppression it is unique, however, in that its nature and particular impact on an individual fluctuates and changes across the life course. The 70-year-old deemed, solely on the basis of chronological age, to be unfit for jury service was once the child told to be 'seen and not heard' and the adolescent whose passion was dismissed as 'puppy love'.

Despite its relevance across the whole of the life course, most discussion of ageism focuses on its place in the lives of older adults. Whilst drawing attention to the prejudice and discrimination experienced by older people, this bias does result in a number of problems. Not only can it serve to bury ageism directed at other age groups, but it can also blind us to ageism within ourselves. Seeing the concept of ageism as relevant only to older adults fosters a 'them' and 'us' view of 'the elderly' as a minority group. If older people are seen as different and separate from the rest of society then this can be used to justify different and separate treatment. Frequently this treatment takes the form of discriminatory practice that restricts the opportunities and services available to older people, although it can also encompass the kindly, but patronising attention – 'keeping an eye on the old dears' – that Johnson and Bytheway (1993) consider the most invidious form of ageism. Johnson and Bytheway (1993) suggest the term 'oldageism' to refer to ageist attitudes and practices specifically directed at older people, with ageism being recognised as a process affecting all individuals from birth onwards, 'at every stage putting limits and constraints on experience, expectations, relationships and opportunities' (Itzin, 1986: 114).

Given the destructive potential of ageism, promulgating the idea of an 'ageless self' (Kaufman, 1986) can be appealing, with age (especially 'old age') consigned to being nothing more than a mask concealing the essential identity of the person beneath (Featherstone and Hepworth, 1989, 1990). However, because ageism is wrong does not mean that age is irrelevant, any more than because sexism and racism are wrong means that gender and race are irrelevant. Thus, Andrews (1999: 309) rails against the concept of agelessness: 'While difference is celebrated in axes such as race, gender, religion and nationality, the same is not true for age. ... [And yet] years are not empty containers:

important things happen in that time. Why must these years be trivialised? They are the stuff of which people's lives are made'. For Andrews, age is an important diversity, with the concept of agelessness being, in effect, itself a form of ageism – this time, through the pretence that age is irrelevant, an underemphasis rather than an overemphasis on its significance. Spinelli (2002), similarly, raises concerns about how the overlooking or denying of general distinctions between child and adult ways of being – in particular with regard to their sexuality – can encourage adult abusers of children to 'convince themselves that their wants and needs (be they of companionship, or sex, or both) are of an equivalent kind and are shared by the very children whose ever more precariously maintained hold on a childhood will be brought to a sudden and infelicitous end by their oppressive acts' (p. 19). These are pleas to recognise the distinctiveness of different life stages.

Whilst ageism is built into the structure of institutions and cultures, it is also internalised in the attitudes of individuals – including counsellors and their clients. A life course perspective provides counsellors with a standpoint from which to examine the impact of age and ageism on themselves, their practice, their clients and the counselling relationship.

Ageism and counselling
Ageism is addressed implicitly in discussions around counselling for children and for older people, but this is not often placed in a life course context. The existence or potentiality for ageism within counselling has received nowhere near the same attention as racism and sexism. Totton (2000), for example in his book *Psychotherapy and Politics*, considers feminist, gay and anti-racist critiques of psychotherapy, but not anti-ageist critiques – perhaps because there isn't really one. Evidence of ageism may be buried within what Totton describes as social critiques – accusations that psychotherapy and counselling frequently minimise the role of material (that is, wealth) and social (that is, class) factors in access to therapy.

Ageism is similar to other forms of oppression in that it rests on one group having access to money and power at the expense of another group (Itzin, 1986). With regard to access to counselling, the power and money reside overwhelmingly with those who are economically most active; namely people in their early and middle adulthood (say between the ages of 25 and 65 years). Pilgrim (1997) raises a rare voice in emphasising the role of age-related power in

influencing who receives counselling and other mental health
services, and for what problems. In this regard, children and older
adults have much in common. It is people in early and middle adulthood who are most likely to be economically active (or potentially
so), whereas the economic power of both the very young and the very
old is frequently either minimal or negative – (although even here
one must be careful since the assumption that older people are
inevitably impoverished is itself an ageist myth). Nonetheless, the very
young and the very old frequently do lack direct economic power and,
as a result, they also lack social power – both of which may be needed
to gain access to appropriate counselling and psychotherapy.

In counselling relationships, the age and life stage of the counsellor in relation to the age and life stage of the client is also relevant.
Clients at a very different life stage to our own may remind us of
who we were (as children) or of who we might become (as elders);
reminders that we may or may not acknowledge and may or may not
welcome, but that will nonetheless influence the counselling relationship and the nature of the counselling that is offered. When
trainee counsellors are asked to explore the question of which age
groups of clients they would feel most and least comfortable working
with (something that you are invited to consider later, in Activity 7:
Working with clients of different ages), many say that, putting aside
the need for special training in order to work with the under 16s,
they would feel most comfortable working with clients of their own
age or younger. It is generally only those who already have considerable experience (not necessarily in a counselling role) of working
with people in late adulthood who express confidence about working with clients considerably older than themselves. Trainees in their
20s may also express doubts about working with midlife clients.
There may be justifiable concerns (Pilgrim, 1997) about whether the
disparity between their own life experience and that of clients of different generations might limit the possibility of developing truly
empathic relationships. Comments may reflect concerns about feeling ignorant or ill-equipped: 'As people and as practitioners we may
feel a sense of audacity or anxiety in sitting down with someone as
much as 40 or 50 years our senior: what can we offer them? How
might they see us? What might they expect or be able to accept from
us?' (Richards, 2001: 12).

So, where does the foregoing discussion leave us in terms of the
rest of the present book? Hopefully it has made the case for the
relevance of counsellors' taking a life course perspective on their

work. Theoretical understandings of the life course can, I believe, provide concepts to be used in the midst of everyday life, and what Egan (1990: 17) refers to as 'the kind of applied understandings that enable helpers to work with clients'. My main aim in writing this book is to foster in readers an awareness of and sensitivity to life course issues that can enhance your capacity for empathy with clients of all ages and life stages; and, secondarily, to achieve this in part by encouraging you to reflect on the relevance of life course issues to your own life.

2

Developmental tasks and themes

'When I was a child, I spake as a child, I understood as a child, I thought as a child: but when I became a man, I put away childish things.'

(The First Epistle of Paul to the Corinthians, xiii, 11)

For most of us, phrases such as the 'terrible twos', the 'adolescent identity crisis', the 'midlife crisis', the 'empty nest syndrome' and the 'twilight years' probably conjure up not dissimilar images. Each of these terms implies a life course with recognisable and recognisably different stages – a path delineated by age-associated experiences and punctuated by age-associated events. But these are very generalised concepts. As a prelude to the following chapter, which focuses on the counselling needs of clients at different life stages, the present chapter considers some concepts for thinking about the stages themselves, and the themes or threads that run through them. One consequence of adopting a life course standpoint is the awareness that it focuses on the issues that bind as well as on those that separate us all (Sugarman and Woolfe, 1997) – in particular, in the present context, clients and helpers. It fosters an awareness that we share common ground (Coles, 1996) and, in keeping with this, the present chapter first asks you to think of your own experience, dividing your life into different chapters, as suggested in Activity 3: Life chapters. For the same reason, the chapter ends with an exploration of themes in life span development through the example of counsellor career development.

Activity 3: Life chapters

In this exercise you are invited, in effect, to begin constructing an autobiography. Based on the interview schedule developed by Dan McAdams (1997) to explore *Stories We Live By*, you are asked to begin this exploration by identifying 'chapters' in your life. The goal is not to give the 'whole story', merely a sense of the story's outline – a table of contents.

Think of your life as if it were a book, with each part of your life comprising a different chapter. Of course, the book is still unfinished, but it probably already contains several interesting and well-defined chapters. Divide your life into its major chapters – say, between two and eight in number – and briefly describe each one. Think of this as a general table of contents for your book. Give each chapter a name and describe its overall contents. Discuss briefly the transition from one chapter to the next.

Although some people find the 'Life chapters' exercise difficult, few find it incomprehensible. Whilst the details may vary, all societies rationalise the passage of time, and divide the life course into socially relevant units – thereby transforming 'biological' time into 'social' time. As I revise this chapter for the final time in February 2003, the British Broadcasting Corporation is about to launch BBC3, its new television channel directed, according to the pre-launch publicity, 'primarily at people in their twenties and thirties'. Such age-banding of our society is not legally determined or enforced, but exists through our tacit assumption and acceptance of age differences. Shakespeare's 'All the world's a stage' speech from *As You Like It*, the nursery rhyme about Solomon Grundy (who was 'Born on Monday, Christened on Tuesday, Married on Wednesday' etc.), and a good number of articles in newspapers and magazines all point to the ubiquitousness of stage-based views of the life course. Each suggests or implies a series of different concerns – or developmental tasks (Havighurst, 1972) – that characterise different life stages.

Developmental tasks

The term 'developmental task' was coined in 1948 by Robert Havighurst (1972), an American educationalist who, amongst other things, strove to identify 'teachable moments' in children's education – points in time when children were especially receptive to particular types of learning. He was also interested in ageing, and advocated an 'activity theory' of successful ageing (Havighurst et al., 1968) – the idea that it is preferable to remain actively involved in society as we move into later adulthood, and not to 'disengage' (Cumming and Henry, 1961; Cumming, 1975) in the manner advocated by the then main competing model of successful ageing. Havighurst's interest in all stages of the life span led to the development of his theory of developmental tasks as the basis of different life stages. It is an idea that is echoed both implicitly and explicitly in the work of many subsequent theorists of change and development across the life course.

The developmental task theory of life stages can be summarised in seven key points.

- A developmental task is 'a task which arises at or about a certain period in the life of the individual, successful achievement of which leads to ... happiness and to success with later tasks, while failure leads to unhappiness in the individual, disapproval by the society, and difficulty with later tasks' (Havighurst, 1972: 2).
- A developmental task is midway between an individual need and a societal demand, assuming an active learner interacting with an active social environment.
- Developmental tasks are the outcome of biological maturation, cultural pressures, and individual desires, aspirations and values. Some tasks will arise primarily from one source, although most arise from the combination of these factors acting together.
- Because of the involvement of individual aspirations and cultural and social norms (all of which vary across people, place and/or time) in the establishment of developmental tasks, the tasks associated with different life stages will vary across individuals, cultures and epochs.
- Because of the involvement of biological and psychological processes that are universal across people, time and place, there will be some commonality of developmental tasks for widely different individuals, families and communities.
- The developmental tasks associated with different life stages operate as a type of culturally specific guidance system. By providing a ready-made set of personal goals, normative developmental tasks can help people make decisions about how to order and manage their lives.

- By the same token, the coercive character of normative developmental tasks can also constrain a person's freedom of choice, and inhibit people's ability to develop alternative, non-normative lifestyles.

Havighurst identified six to nine developmental tasks for each of six age periods ranging from 'Infancy and early childhood' to 'Later maturity'. His recognition of the impact on developmental tasks of social, cultural and historical change and difference led him to revise and update his list several times during his career. Focusing on broader-based psychological preoccupations of different life stages rather than on concrete developmental tasks increases the chances of identifying stages that are more generalisable across time and place. This is the level of analysis in Erikson's stage-based theory of development across the life span. In what still remains one of the most widely cited theories of psychosocial development, Erikson distinguished eight developmental stages, beginning with infancy and ending with old age. The main elements of his theory of life span development can be summarised in ten key points.

- Development is a *psychosocial* process – both internal psychological factors and external social factors are involved.
- As individuals develop they must adapt to new demands that society imposes on them.
- These demands occur according to the *epigenetic* principle – a term borrowed from embryology asserting that 'anything that grows has a ground plan, and out of this ground plan the parts arise, each part having its time of special ascendency, until all forms have arisen to form a functioning whole' (Erikson, 1980: 53).
- The need to respond to this sequential series of demands leads to a series of *psychosocial crises* for the individual.
- Although each demand has its 'time of special ascendency', it is not absent from other points of the life course. This is perhaps the most frequently overlooked aspect of Erikson's theory.
- How well and completely people cope with the demands of a given stage determines towards which of two poles they migrate – one representing positive and the other negative development.
- Development is cumulative and increasingly complex. As each new task is addressed earlier resolutions are also questioned.
- Resolution of the demands of a particular stage is never absolute – a *'favourable ratio'* of positive to negative resolution is the goal.

- Successful resolution of the tasks of a particular stage leads to the development of a new *virtue* or *vital strength* within the individual that is also manifested within a culture's social institutions.
- Any psychosocial crisis that is not successfully resolved leaves a residue that interferes with later tasks.

The ages that typically mark the boundaries between stages are, at times, very rough approximations. Whilst there is general agreement that the first crisis is primarily an issue of the first year of life, from the end of the second stage onwards different age boundaries have been suggested for all stages, particularly for those of the adult years. This variation occurs because the developmental periods are partially defined by the society in which the person lives. A particular period may begin, for example, when a child begins formal education. In a society where formal education is delayed, the timing of the developmental stage may also be affected. By the time we reach adulthood, the immense variation in our experience, the wide range of possible routes through the adult years, and the greater influence of social and cultural relative to biological factors, results in the age norms associated with adulthood being less rigid than those of the childhood years. It is to be expected, therefore, that there will be wider variation in the onset and timing of the stages beyond adolescence. Erikson's model is not, therefore, a model of stages based primarily on age. Erikson's psychosocial stages are generally labelled via the bipolar alternatives that represent successful and unsuccessful resolution of each crisis. Since, however, in reality resolution is not so clear-cut one way or the other, nor is it complete and never to be returned to, Erikson's stages are represented in Table 2.1 as a sequence of issues that tend to dominate a particular point in the life course, but will both be implicated ahead of their 'time of special ascendency' and continue to have significance once their moment at centre stage is past.

Despite variations in the nature and significance of particular developmental tasks even for people of similar age and background, it is possible to identify a number of tasks that are associated, at least to some extent, with particular ages and/or life stages. The next Activity Trail exercise, Activity 4: Developmental stages and tasks, explores this point. Whilst some of this age grading of society may be enshrined by law and formal regulation, much is grounded primarily in custom and practice. As we grow up we tend to internalise the age norms of our society, developing largely taken-for-granted assumptions about the type, timing and sequence of major milestones

Table 2.1 *Erikson's stages of life span development*

Approximate age	Issues centre around
0–1 years	*Trust* – the confidence that one's basic needs will be met
1–6	*Autonomy* – self-control without loss of self-esteem
6–10	*Purpose* – the initiative to strive for goals that will fulfil personal potential
10–14	*Competence* – acquisition of the skills needed for full and productive involvement in society
14–20	*Identity* – developing an integrated self-concept and a coherent set of values and beliefs
20–35	*Intimacy* – the establishment of close, committed relationships with others
35–65	*Generativity* – the creation of a lasting contribution that will extend beyond one's own lifetime
65+	*Integrity* – acceptance of and satisfaction with one's life, and the understanding of its place as part of a wider humanity

that will mark out our life course. Being 'on time' or 'off time' for these events typically provides a compelling basis for self-evaluation.

Activity 4: Developmental stages and tasks

We cannot live the afternoon of life according to the program of life's morning, for what in the morning was true will at evening be a lie. Whoever carries into the afternoon the law of the morning ... must pay with damage to his soul.

(Jung, 1972)

If you were to divide the life course into a series of stages:

- Where would you place the boundaries between stages?
- What would mark the boundaries between different stages?
- What would you call each stage?
- What are the key features of each stage in terms of:
  - main tasks and priorities for the individual;
  - societal expectations;
  - major roles.

If possible, spend some time thinking about these questions on your own, and then work in a small group to address the questions more systematically. When you think about each life stage it is sometimes helpful to have one or two particular individuals in mind, as well as thinking in generalities. The previous activity, Activity 3: Life chapters, was, of course, asking not dissimilar questions about your own life course.

The developmental tasks associated with a particular age or life stage will have a significant impact on the concerns that clients bring to counselling. Even when individuals are 'on target' – that is, working on the resolution of developmental tasks typically associated with their age and life stage – counselling input and support may be indicated. Because a person is addressing the issues and tasks 'typical' of someone in their position does not mean that the task is necessarily easy or straightforward. Even deciding what constitutes age-appropriate behaviour can be difficult. Our view of the 'normal, expectable life cycle' (Neugarten, 1979), develops well before we actually live it out, and changing social conditions may render it outdated and no longer accurate. A role for counsellors may, therefore, be to help clients let go of outdated assumptions about age norms. Some clients will mourn their loss, and find it hard to formulate new life goals and alternative criteria of self-worth. Others will more readily find it liberating.

Many counselling services and practices enshrine, at least implicitly, aspects of a stage-based theory of the life course. Services are often organised around provision for clients of particular ages or life stages and the developmental tasks characteristic of that point in the life course. In so doing, these services both reflect and contribute to the reality of sequential life stages. Like other stage theories, Erikson's model can be used 'as a template to locate possible sources of personal difficulty' (Jacobs, 1998: 11), giving the counsellor what Thomas (1990: 19) describes as 'a head start in working with clients ... [by providing] some initial expectations or probabilities which then can be confirmed, revised, or rejected' in the light of the experience of working with any one particular client.

Age norms – particularly for the adult years – are undoubtedly less rigid and compelling than in the past, bringing uncertainty and loss of direction. Even back in 1976, Neugarten and Hagestad commented on the increasing fluidity of the adult years of the life cycle, with increasing numbers of transitions, the disappearance of traditional timetables, and the lack of synchrony among age-related roles:

> Entry into the labor market comes later; exit, earlier. Marriage, parenthood, and grandparenthood are differently timed. Increasing numbers of men and women marry, divorce, then remarry, care for children in two-parent, then one-parent, then two-parent households, enter and re-enter the labor force, change jobs, undertake new careers or return to school. (p. 35)

It has become a truism that such variability is increasing rather than decreasing:

> People are becoming detraditionalized, nomadized, 'casualized,' as the old fixed points of reference disappear. Instead of marriage, a series of relationships; instead of a home, a series of addresses; instead of a career, freelancing; instead of a church, the irregularly mushrooming politics of protest; instead of a faith, what ever one is currently 'into'; instead of stable identities, pluralism and flux; instead of society, the market and one's own circle. (Cupitt, 1997: 74)

However, despite this fragmentation of the life course and disintegration of many previous near-certainties, age norms have not totally disappeared, and counsellors will see clients concerned that their life course experiences are in some way 'out of step' with social norms and expectations about the timing of life events. Age norms give a degree of structure and predictability to the life course, providing signposts for individual aspirations and markers for developmental deadlines (Schutz and Heckhausen, 1996; Heckhausen, 1999). Internalised assumptions about age-appropriate behaviour, combined with social pressure to conform to prevailing age norms can make being 'off time' uncomfortable and difficult, often leading to negative self-assessments. Counsellors may need to explore with clients the extent to which their age-related aspirations and evaluations reflect social expectations rather than personal goals. This is complicated by the 'concealed' or 'hidden' nature of many socially constructed definitions of age-appropriate behaviour, such that clients may experience such norms as 'natural' (that is, universal and in-born), seeing discrepancy between these norms and their own achievements as personal failings. Counsellors can explore with clients the boundaries between what is and is not changeable, and the extent to which age norms and expectations need not be as restrictive as they might at first appear.

However, the psychological themes and preoccupations that make up the developmental tasks of different life stages do not arise at precise moments in life, each to be tidily addressed and resolved 'as if it were a bead on a chain' (Neugarten, 1982: 369). Thus, whilst considerations of life stage haunt both theories of change and access to counselling across the life course, they are by no means the whole story. Especially with regard to the years beyond adolescence, life stages are to a significant degree artifice and fiction.

Real life is less regulated than the existence of age-related developmental tasks may suggest. We take stock of our life, assessing our successes and failures, reviewing our hopes and aspirations, and reformulating our life goals. These, indeed, are the defining features of the structure-changing phases in the evolution of a life structure. Through this process identity is formed and reformed. Issues of attachment, dependency, autonomy, intimacy, communication, co-operation, conflict, and power and control re-emerge as recurring and cyclical themes in our lives (Jacobs, 1998; Noller et al., 2000). The repeated emergence and re-emergence of these developmental themes provides an adjunct to a stage-based view of developmental tasks across the life course.

Developmental themes

Think for a moment of a long, stripy, painstakingly woven scarf. Each stripe is a different colour; representing a particular life stage. The green is, perhaps, middle childhood; the red – adolescence; and the purple – late adulthood. We can recognise the different stripes, even though every scarf is slightly different – some stripes are wider than others; no two blues, browns or yellows are quite the same hue; and sometimes there is variation in the weave. However, not only are the stripes recognisable, but they are joined to each other by threads that run throughout the whole scarf – the yarn onto which the wool is woven. It is these threads that hold the scarf together, and represent themes or continuities that run through the whole garment.

The next Activity Trail exercise (Activity 5: Lifeline) is a starting point for accessing the recurrent themes that wend their way through the life course. It is, perhaps, the most ubiquitous structured exercise in the field of life course development. It forms part of many career and life goal planning workshops, is included in many access-to-education programmes, and may form a prelude to life story work with disparate groups, including those in self-help support groups, drug abuse rehabilitation groups and inmate education programmes within prisons. Doubtless, many of you will have completed a Lifeline exercise at least once, and may use it in your work with clients. Instructions and precise format may vary – but the version shown in Activity 5 is fairly typical.

Activity 5: Lifeline

Take a blank sheet of paper and, allowing the left- and right-hand edges of the page to represent the beginning and end of your life respectively, draw, in the manner of a temperature chart, a line across the page to depict the peaks and troughs experienced in your life so far, and those you would predict for the future.

When finished, sit back and ask yourself some questions about this graph – your 'lifeline'.

- What is its general shape? Does it continue to rise throughout life? Does it depict peaks and troughs around some arbitrary mean? Alternatively, is there a plateau and subsequent fall in the level of the curve? Is it punctuated with major or only relatively minor peaks and troughs?
- The horizontal axis represents time; but how about the vertical axis – what dimension does that reflect?
- What (or who) triggered the peaks and troughs in the graph? Why did they occur at the time that they did?
- What might have been done (or was done) to make the peaks higher and the troughs shallower? How might the incidence and height of the peaks be increased in the future? And the incidence and depth of the troughs decreased?
- What positive results emerged from the troughs and what were the negative consequences of the peaks?

Fundamental to the Lifeline exercise is the idea that our past, present and future are all inexorably linked. I don't recall anyone having produced an 'interrupted' Lifeline, where the line stops suddenly and then restarts in a different place. Despite the multifarious highs, lows and significant events or turning points within a Lifeline, the graph also accommodates continuity and, specifically, themes within the life course. But what themes to focus on? Even more than with the question of the possible basis of life stages, the seeker of life themes is spoilt for choice. In part it is a question, as the saying goes, of 'horses for courses' – it depends on why you want to disentangle themes. Developmental psychologists (who, traditionally, have focused primarily on infancy and childhood) typically distinguish (for example, Rice, 2001) between physical, cognitive, personal and social development. Counsellors may find that adjusting to physical development or decline may be an issue for some clients, and, especially when working with children and adolescents, account must be taken of the client's stage of cognitive development. However, in the counselling setting, it is aspects of personal and social (or interpersonal) development – the shifting balance between dependence, interdependence and autonomy– that are most likely to echo through the ages (Jacobs, 1998).

To underscore the relevance of developmental tasks and themes to the lives of counsellors as well as to their clients, the spotlight turns in the following section, as in several of the Activity Trail exercises, to the counsellor rather than the client, and considers the process of becoming and being a counsellor as a long-term life course issue rather than a point-in-time decision.

Stages in counsellors' professional development

The route into becoming a counsellor or psychotherapist is generally circuitous (Norcross and Guy, 1989), and counselling cannot be a profession that is entered into lightly, or without thought. Selection procedures, with their requirements for prior experience, self-reflection and explanation, more or less preclude this. That both personal and professional development do not end with the attainment of a diploma, or even with accreditation by a respected professional body, is acknowledged through the importance accorded to supervision and to continued professional development. Adopting a life course perspective provides a framework for considering the professional development of counsellors both during training and beyond the point of qualification. Activity 6 sets the scene for this deliberation.

Activity 6: Curriculum vitae

The career and life stage of the counsellor, as well as the life stage of the client, is a significant factor in the counselling relationship. Take a while to reflect on the following questions that look back to your entry into the counselling profession, and also tap into what your future in counselling might be like.

- When did I decide to become a counsellor? Can I identify a particular point in time, or a particular formative experience?
- Why did I enter the profession at the point in my life that I did?
- To what extent has my experience of the profession turned out in the way I expected it to?
- How different (assuming your experience goes back that far) a counsellor am I now from how I was two, five, ten years ago?
- Now imagine your future in counselling. In five years' time ..., in ten years' time. ... What will I be doing?

  - What tasks?
  - What clients?
  - What settings?
  - What achievements?
  - What aspirations?
  - What concerns?

- Will I be a better counsellor?
- How will I know?

As a follow-up to this activity – and linking back to Activity 1: Metaphors of the life course, and forward to Chapter 5: Life stories – you might think about the different ways that you could tell the story of your career:

- First, imagine you are telling your story to a *close friend* you have not seen for a long time – a person, who, in the past, you shared confidences with, who you trust, and who you feel knows you well.
- Next, imagine you are telling your story to a *potential employer*, someone who you have not met before, but who is in the position to offer you the job of your dreams.
- What would be the similarities and differences between the two versions of your career story? Why might they be different? What does this tell you about how you present yourself in different settings?
- How might clients choose to present their story to you when you first meet? How might this change during the course of counselling?

Theories of occupational choice and development have been around for some considerable time, encapsulated in the stages and sub-stages proposed by Donald Super (1957; Super et al., 1988):

- exploration (crystallisation, specification, implementation);
- establishment (stabilisation, consolidation, advancement);
- maintenance (holding, updating, innovating); and
- disengagement (deceleration, retirement planning, retirement living).

However, as the occupational world has become more diverse and volatile, so single-strand, ladder-like theories of career development have become less tenable even for the middle-class professional occupations that they might once have reflected. Sometimes the sequence is telescoped into a shorter time frame – whereby a person passes through the stages of exploration, establishment, maintenance and disengagement several times in a working life marked by one or more significant changes of direction. It is, indeed, likely that this is the pattern for many of you, with your career in counselling following on from employment in other lines of work. Super (1980, 1990) also broadened the scope of his theory beyond the area of paid employment by embracing, in the form of a 'Life-Career Rainbow', a 'total life-span, total life-space' view of the life course. Here he distinguished major roles that most people will occupy in the course of their life (including child, citizen, homemaker, leisure user, parent, student, spouse and worker) and identified as significant variables their time demands and their emotional significance.

With regard to the field of counselling and psychotherapy, Skovholt and Ronnestad (1995) list 15 models of professional development – and this does not include their own. Many of these models concentrate primarily on the early years of a therapist's career, with particular emphasis on initial training. Thus, Stoltenberg and Delworth (1987) distinguish four levels of therapist professional development, three of which are trainee level and one is that of the 'Integrated Counsellor'. This mirrors the emphasis in the earliest theories of occupational choice on the point of initial career choice and entry – perhaps reflecting an implicit assumption that once this choice had been made – once the deed was done, as it were – the rest of a person's working life would stretch before them in a predictable and possibly immutable way.

Skovholt and Ronnestad (1995) extend the span of attention to the whole of a therapist's professional career and present a model based on qualitative data gleaned from interviews with over 100 therapists, ranging from those yet to begin formal training to those on the verge of retirement after a long professional career. The stages that they identified (see Table 2.2) are presented as 'conceptually and structurally flexible and porous' (p. 13) rather than rigid; and are recognised as abstractions that cannot encapsulate all the nuances of individual experience. Only the barest of details are given in Table 2.2, but it does serve to illustrate what Fear and Woolfe (1999) identify as a fundamental theme in counsellors' ongoing professional development – namely, a

Table 2.2 *The stages of professional counsellor development (Skovholt and Ronnestad, 1995)*

Timing	Stage	Central task
Pre-training	*Conventional*	Use what one has learned as a friend, family member, neighbour or work associate etc.
Early training	*Transition to professional training*	Assimilate information from many sources and apply it during skills training
Intermediate training	*Imitation of experts*	Maintain openness to information and theory whilst modelling in practice the behaviour and style of experts
Full-time supervised practice*	*Conditional autonomy*	Become socialised into the field and function at an established, professional level
2–5 years post-qualification	*Exploration*	Explore beyond what is known, anchoring theoretical and conceptual structures to one's own value base
The next 2–5 years	*Integration*	Develop a professional authenticity that includes a conceptual system and working style which is true to oneself
The next 10–30 years	*Individuation*	Highly individualised and idiosyncratic growth leading to a deeper authenticity
The next 1–10 years	*Integrity*	Maintain the fullness of one's individuality while also preparing for retirement

*Note that these stages are premised on the North American model of training that typically comprises a full-time graduate programme, followed by an internship lasting up to two years.

process of working towards the integration of philosophy and practice. Skovholt and Ronnestad (1995) identify this growth towards professional individuation as the first and overriding theme in counsellor professional development.

Professional development as growth towards professional individuation

Professional individuation involves a gradually increasing integration of the professional self and the personal self. It includes consistency between therapists' ideology (their values and theoretical stance) and the methods and techniques used in their practice. Although it is an expression of deeper and deeper layers of the self, the process is, in Skovholt and Ronnestad's (1995) words, 'saturated with relationships' (p. 101). Clients, peers, professional elders, family, friends and supervisors all have an impact. It leads towards a point where, 'within an ethical and competent context, the individual freely chooses the framework and form of professional functioning' (Skovholt and Ronnestad, 1995: 101).

The road to professional individuation is neither smooth nor straightforward. It includes a movement from an unarticulated, pre-conceptual way of functioning where, because of this lack of insight, little distinction is made between the personal realm and the professional realm – 'helping' and personal relationships may be largely indistinguishable. With regard to the stages of skills acquisition this can be seen as the stage of unconscious incompetence (Robinson, 1974) – 'Not knowing what it is I do not know'.

Professional training changes all that. As trainees undergo their long period of immersion, instruction and socialisation into (in the terms of the British Association for Counselling and Psychotherapy) a core theoretical model, it is necessary to meet the approval of powerful professional gatekeepers in training establishments and professional bodies (especially those with powers of accreditation and sanction). The struggle to achieve the externally imposed modes of functioning that are deemed professionally appropriate can open up a gulf between trainees' pretraining personal functioning and their developing professional self. Professional functioning becomes more externally driven, and, as characteristic personal methods of functioning are suppressed, individuals may show greater rigidity with regard to working style and conceptual analysis. This is the stage of conscious incompetence and the consequent struggle for conscious competence, 'I know what I don't know and am trying to do what I know I ought'.

This is, however, far from the end of the road. The disparity that develops between the person and their developing professional self will be addressed in the personal development aspect of training, although it is likely to be many years post-training – in the integrity stage (see Table 2.2) – before it is fully breached. Integral to this process of professional individuation is an increasing reliance on and confidence in internal rather than external authority. Conceptual systems and working style become increasingly congruent with the personal self. They become more nuanced and unique. It embodies the process of becoming more the self that one truly is

(Rogers, 1967). Rowan (1994) likens it to the process of discovering, catching, taming and leaving behind a powerful bull – a Buddist metaphor of spiritual development.

In their book, Skovholt and Ronnestad offer the distillation of interviews with over 100 counsellors and therapists. In other studies counsellors speak for themselves. Thus, Dryden and Spurling (1989) edit autobiographical accounts of 'the personal and professional journeys' (Norcross and Guy, 1989: 215) of 10 prominent psychotherapists, and Goldfried (2001b) the accounts of 15 (also prominent) therapists concerning how they changed during the course of their professional lives. Goldfried found that, like himself, the 15 therapists moved, with time, to a more integrative theoretical position. Clinical experience, he concluded, 'can soften the sharp theoretical differences often seen in less experienced therapists' (2001a: 329). Like Skovholt and Ronnestad, the stories he records show therapists originally learning, in effect, what they are taught. Subsequently, and generally in a supportive and understanding interpersonal context, ways of functioning that are not, or are not any longer, effective can be recognised and modified, leading to the process of individuation described by Skovholt and Ronnestad. The titles of some of the autobiographical accounts give the flavour of this journey: 'How I learned to abandon certainty and embrace change' (Stricker, 2001); 'From insight and reflection to action and clinical breadth' (Lazarus, 2001); 'My change process: from certainty through chaos to complexity' (Greenberg, 2001). These examples come, respectively, from the three theoretical 'stables' from which Goldfried's contributors originally emanated – the psychodynamic, the cognitive-behavioural and the experiential.

It must, of course, be remembered that Goldfried's book is by and about therapists who have come to see themselves as self-confessed integrative or eclectic practitioners. Even when this is not the case (for example, in the professional autobiographies recounted in Dryden and Spurling, 1989) there is still the sense of personal integration and professional individuation. Thus Norcross and Guy (1989), in attempting an overview of the themes emerging from these autobiographical accounts, comment on the effort made to distinguish the receipt of a formal qualification and accreditation from 'the individual and emotional acceptance of the calling' (p. 228). 'The latter', they go on to say, 'typically occurs many, many moons after the former. ... It hardly seems possible to become a sophisticated therapist in less than ten years; these therapists' odysseys poignantly attest to the gradual process of professional maturation' (p. 228).

The end of this chapter marks the return to a focus on the client rather than the counsellor. This does not, however, take us into a totally separate arena. Goldfried notes how the therapists' experience of change closely parallels the ways in which clients change during therapy:

> Within a supportive interpersonal context, the person becomes aware of things in one's life that are remnants of the past and do not necessarily work in the current situation. With the encouragement and support of others, he or she is exposed to new learning situations that provide the kind of corrective experiences that alter how one emotionally, cognitively, and behaviorally approaches various events. This is how our clients change and how many of us as therapists change. (p. 326)

3

Counselling across the life course

'*The trials of life: Spills; Drills; Thrills; Bills; Ills; Pills; Wills.*'

(Anon.)

It is easy for our knowledge and expertise to become insular. Even to keep on top of developments relating to counselling with clients of the age and life stage that we encounter most frequently – be this primary school children, adolescents, university students, mid-career managers, retirees, the frail elderly, etc. – can be daunting. Finding the time and opportunity to look beyond the parapet and into the terrain of other counsellors' work can be even harder. This chapter offers a glimpse into these other worlds by forming the concerns of disparate client groups into some sort of coherent whole under the umbrella of the life course. By way of introduction to this topic, the next post on our putative Activity Trail – Activity 7: Working with clients of different ages – suggests questions for reflection that can provide a background to this analysis.

Activity 7: Working with clients of different ages

In the counselling encounter the lives of client and counsellor touch each other at particular points in the life cycle of each. Each will be working, both inside and outside the counselling relationship, implicitly and explicitly, and with varying degrees of ease and success, on his or her developmental

> *tasks. ... This view of the life cycle is like a glue which binds together the experience of the helper and the client, and of the disparate concerns raised by clients at different life stages.*
>
> *(Sugarman and Woolfe, 1997)*

You may be just embarking on your career in counselling, or you may have many years of experience – so obviously there will be variation in the range of clients you have worked with. As with all exercises in the Activity Trail, the questions below are triggers for reflection, and it is assumed that you will adapt them as necessary to your own circumstances.

- What has been the age range of clients you have worked with?
- How does the age of the client influence the way that you work? What varies and what remains the same?
- Setting aside the requirement for specific training for work with the under-16s, what ages of clients would you feel happy working with, even if you do not currently do so?
- What ages of clients would you not want to work with? Why?

Many micro-skills are common to counselling with clients of all ages (Geldard and Geldard, 1999) and many significant life events that might bring clients into counselling – bereavement, illness, traumatic stress, for example – have no special or very clear association with age or life stage. Nonetheless, if the differences between counselling children, adolescents and adults are ignored, the outcomes may be disappointing (Geldard and Geldard, 1999). The present chapter, therefore, addresses some of the specific issues concerned with counselling clients at different life stages. Separated out for reasons of convenience and manageability (viz. the dictum: 'eat your elephant a spoonful at a time'), it needs to be remembered that these stages overlap chronologically and, to an even greater extent, psychologically and developmentally. Nonetheless, the following approximate age boundaries are suggested as useful distinctions for considering issues of counselling across the life course.

- *Infancy* – the first 24–30 months of life.
- *Childhood* – up until the age of about 12 years.
- *Adolescence* – between the ages of, approximately, 12 and 18 years.
- *Fledgling adulthood* – 18–25 years.
- *Young adulthood* – 25–40 years.

- *Middle adulthood* – 40–65 years.
- *Late adulthood* – 65 years and beyond.

Now would be a good moment to look back to the developmental phases and tasks you identified in Activity 4, and also the commentary on this exercise in the Appendix. Doubtless, a case could be made for somewhat different age boundaries; boundaries that, in any case, are rarely clear-cut. Many people feel themselves 'betwixt and between' different life stages, having a foot in two camps as it were. It must be remembered that whilst life stage labels have their use, their importance is overshadowed by the need to keep to the fore the individuality and uniqueness of each particular client. The goal is to help clients 'be themselves' rather than 'act their age'.

Counselling with children

Whilst the first two years of life are of crucial importance developmentally, counsellors would generally work with the infant's carers rather than directly with clients of this age. This is counselling *about* rather than *with* children and may even begin before birth, with, for example, the exploration with pregnant women of how their own behaviour during pregnancy may affect the development of their unborn child. However, as children grow beyond infancy and encounter both normative and non-normative events that tax their coping resources, they can increasingly become the direct rather than vicarious recipients of counselling. Children referred for counselling might (Thomas, 1990) include those:

- who have become distraught as the result of a traumatic event within the family or immediate community;
- who suffer a physical disability or an illness that affects their appearance, their ability to engage in the typical activities of their age group, and their feelings of self-worth;
- who do not meet expected developmental milestones with regard to a range of criteria such as toilet training, language development, control of emotions (especially anger and frustration) or social development;
- whose academic progress falls behind that of the majority of their peers;
- who display to an excessive degree characteristics such as depression, cruelty, shyness, aggression, self-deprecation, disdain for others' rights, lack of self-confidence, fear, anger, weeping, etc.;

■ who have been referred as a result of their suffering abuse or neglect at the hands of parents or guardians.

It is crucial that counselling with children takes account of their developmental capacities. Many normative events coincide at least in a rough-and-ready fashion with the child's developmental readiness. Thus, beginning nursery school at the age of three years coincides with the child's increasing ability to tolerate extended separation from primary and intimate carers (Downey, 2003). Similarly, the timing of the transition to primary school and, later, to secondary school coincides with normative stages of cognitive development. This denotes and leads to educational practices geared to the child's level of functioning. Similar considerations need to be made when counselling children. Furthermore, children's response to life events, such as the experience of parental separation or divorce, which may occur at any age, will vary according to their age and stage of cognitive, emotional and social development.

Downey (2003) summarises the special considerations involved in working with children. Of crucial importance is the recognition that the assumption of personal autonomy and of the capacity to choose at the level of individual action, on which counselling with adults is generally based, may not hold. Autonomy and choice require 'the capacity to render one's own behaviour, thoughts and feelings the subject of personal examination ... [and also] the capacity to "step outside" one's own intimate social context in order that relationships, shared beliefs and meanings can also be examined' (Downey, 2003: 325). These capacities are not in-born; they are gradually emerging developmental acquisitions. It cannot be assumed, therefore, that children have the developmental capacity to recognise the purpose of counselling. Furthermore, it means that therapeutic interventions will probably need to be more varied, less verbal and more action-oriented than will generally be the case in work with adults.

A life course perspective lends itself well to the consideration of the social context in which the client is embedded and to the 'dynamic and reciprocal relationships between children and their environment' (Downey, 2003: 328). Children's dependence on carers (generally family members) and others (such as teachers) with responsibilities towards them has a number of implications. First, it means that children are rarely self-referred. It is adults such as parents, teachers or health visitors, concerned about children's behavioural deviations, emotional reactions or developmental delays, who refer them to counsellors, psychologists and psychotherapists (Pilgrim, 1997). This raises questions about the child's motivation for therapeutic work and for their understanding or acceptance of the purpose of the counselling. A second, and perhaps even more significant, implication of children's dependent status is that they are not usually in a position, either practically or psychologically, to 'leave' their primary social contexts. Involvement in the treatment process of significant others in a child's social network – most frequently the parents – is almost inevitable. Indeed, it may be that, in effect, the parents are the counsellors' key clients, with attention focused on the parent–child dyad and on how changes in the parents' behaviour may promote and encourage positive changes in the child. But if parents are unable or unwilling to see the problem in the family context it may be (Houts et al., 1985) that individual work with the child is the only option. In sum, questions of power – or, perhaps more particularly, the client's lack of power – are of crucial importance in therapeutic work with children.

Counselling with adolescents

Whilst the assumption that adolescence is inevitably a tempestuous period of 'storm and stress' vastly overstates the case (Rutter et al., 1976), it is true that adolescence is a stage of life where storm and stress are more likely to occur than at other ages (Arnett, 1999). In the transition from the dependence of childhood to the independence, autonomy and maturity of adulthood the young person faces many biological, cognitive, psychological and social challenges (Geldard and Geldard, 1999). It is often a difficult period of life (Buchanan et al., 1990) characterised by conflict with parents and other authority figures; more mood swings and extremes of emotion (including depression) than either children or adults; and higher rates of risk behaviour – including recklessness, norm-breaking and anti-social behaviour (Arnett, 1999). Adolescents who are sent for counselling, or come of their own accord, are often those (Thomas, 1990; Geldard and Geldard, 1999):

- who suffer mental, physical or social difficulties that cause them problems of self-acceptance and interfere with their academic and social development;
- who are involved in risk-taking and/or anti-social behaviour – including shoplifting, illicit drug or alcohol use, bullying, violence, joyriding, vandalism and/or the carrying of weapons;

- who lag behind peers in school achievement, and need help in coping with their learning difficulties;
- who are in frequent conflict with their parents and/or other family members;
- who need guidance in making educational and other career decisions;
- whose sexual attitudes, behaviour or concerns have brought them to the counsellor for help – clients may include pregnant teenagers, those suffering from sexually transmitted diseases, and those concerned or confused about their sexual identity (in a homophobic society, consistent attraction to and interest in people of the same gender as themselves may make young people feel out of step with their peers and give rise to anxiety; Mabey and Sorensen, 1995)

Adolescence is 'a permanently shifting sand' (Mabey and Sorensen, 1995) during which clients may present varied and complex problems. However, it is also the case that most young people survive adolescence without much damage (Rutter et al., 1976). In the passage through this period distinction must be made between what is normal and in accordance with the life stage and what is deviant. Counsellors need to be able to accept uncritically behaviours such as changeability (including the tendency to change tack or switch topics during conversations) and unreliability that are developmentally normal during adolescence (Geldard and Geldard, 1999).

Whilst adolescence can be distinguished as a life stage in its own right, its place in the life course between childhood and adulthood is also important. Counselling and therapy with young adolescents (approximately the ages between 12 and 14 years) can have many similarities to work with children. Thus, like children, young adolescents rarely self-refer and, again, parents are almost always involved either directly or indirectly in the therapy. Often young adolescents will regard counsellors as an extension of their parents, or as additional authority figures alongside teachers, doctors, social workers, police officers or other adults with whom they have had dealings. Counsellors cannot assume, therefore, that their independence and client-centredness is recognised or accepted by their adolescent clients. Young clients may have concerns about the boundaries of confidentiality and may feel the relationship lacks the privacy necessary for significant self-disclosure (Geldard and Geldard, 1999).

Young adolescents live mainly in the present, and often find it both difficult and uncongenial to reflect on their actions and inner experiences. As in work with children, counselling may need to be more active and direct than is usual with adults. An adolescent's self-concept is just beginning to take shape and is still somewhat unstable, so therapists can guide their clients in the exploration of possibilities and impossibilities, being both a model and a parental figure as well as a 'congruent and transparent other' (Geertjens and Waaldijk, 1998: 159). However, active directiveness may not be appropriate. If adolescent clients resent the often high level of adult intrusion that they experience in their lives, they may withdraw into silence or uncooperativeness as their only way of maintaining a sense of personal integrity (Mabey and Sorensen, 1995). Furthermore, they may find it difficult to believe that they will be listened to, or that their opinions, beliefs, perceptions and feelings will be accepted as valid.

Cognitive development – in particular the refinement of abstract thinking – develops throughout the teenage years, and by late adolescence (say, the ages of 17 to 18 or 19) clients become increasingly able to engage in the reflective thought more typical of work with adults. However, clients of this age may still perceive even young counsellors as authority figures. This can accentuate their feelings of dependency, making it hard for them to be in counselling when their conscious aspirations are towards autonomy and independence (Geertjens and Waaldijk, 1998).

Counselling with fledgling adults

Although those between the ages of 18 and 25 are often referred to as young adults, this may, by implying that the status of adulthood has been reached, be somewhat misleading. Think back to your responses to Activity 2: What is an adult? and to the commentary in the Appendix. If you think of the range of different minimum age legislation that exists – for voting, for criminal responsibility, for marriage, for joining the armed forces, for the age of consent, for obtaining a driving licence – it is hardly surprising that the onset of adulthood is beset with confusion. It is a status acquired haphazardly and little by little. To be sure, young people in the 18–25-year age band are legally adults, but this does not mean that they feel 'grown up'. They move towards adulthood in the context of a diminishing support network (Apter, 2002), and this can leave them feeling isolated and vulnerable. Contact with parents and other relatives may diminish or be lost as family ties weaken or disintegrate through divorce, geographic dispersion and social diversity. Friendship networks may be unstable. They are less likely to have strong religious affiliation. Universities no longer operate *in loco parentis*.

The dynamic, fluid and transitional quality of this period is captured in such terms as emerging (Arnett, 2000), threshold (Apter, 2001, 2002) or fledgling adulthood. Like adolescence, it is a stage that is culturally constructed – and during the last three decades of the twentieth century it became a period of increasing demographic diversity and instability. There are now no certainties, and ever fewer probabilities, in relation to likely occupational, residential, marital or parental status. Thus, for example, whilst many 18–22-year-olds are in full-time higher education – allowing student counselling to become a distinct and well-defined area of work – many others are not.

Life stage issues that fledgling adults may bring to counselling (Thomas, 1990; Cooper, 2003) include:

- difficulties occurring in relation to family and friends;
- issues of sexual identity and development;
- questions of morality in the face of an imperfect self and a flawed society;
- problems of planning a career, finding satisfactory employment and adjusting to job conditions;
- financial difficulties.

Whilst these difficulties and their manifestations are by no means unique to the period of fledgling adulthood, the developmental status and social demands of this stage lend them a particular quality and form. The shift in gaze from family to peers offers freedom, but can also engender anxiety if such distancing from parents is perceived as risking the loss of their love and support. Furthermore, the independence that a job or full-time education away from home can bestow may be compromised by continued financial dependence on parents, and by the need to return to the family fold if subsequent occupational opportunities fail to materialise, or the cost of housing outstrips their income. This is the 'boomerang' generation – they leave home but (sometimes to the discomfiture of their parents) keep coming back. If, in contrast, their professional and/or financial success seems set to outstrip that of their parents, they may feel they are in some way being disloyal and be unable to grasp the opportunities before them (Cooper, 2003).

Fledgling adults will often be concerned with establishing a workable and acceptable system of values – it is a time for putting into practice (or not) the idealism of adolescence. Awareness of the discrepancies between their own pretensions and performances can be acute, with assessment of their own and other people's moral standards being largely grounded in the quality of personal relationships (Cooper, 2003). The fledgling adult anticipates that, largely through various social and sexual experiences, the unstable and ill-defined self-concept of adolescence will become more clear and consolidated, and that a specific and fixed sexual identity will be established. Whilst this may be true to some degree, the plasticity of human development – including sexual orientation (Rivers, 1997) – is easily underestimated. The myth of adulthood as a fixed and stable state is pervasive, and distorts both expectations and self-evaluations of personal success and failure.

As fledgling adults strive towards adulthood, the ripples of their struggle disturb the equanimity and sense of being 'in charge' of the generation ahead of them. It emphasises to parents that they are growing older, and that the society they created will eventually be supplanted and overtaken by this new generation. The majority of counsellors will still be a good many years older than their fledgling adult clients, and so intergenerational dynamics will again be an issue in the client–counsellor relationship. Counsellors may at times find that their world-view more closely approximates that of the parents than of the fledgling adults themselves.

Counselling with young adults

By their mid-20s most fledgling adults will have largely achieved the outer trappings of separation from their family of origin. Life will have lost some of its 'provisional' character (Levinson et al., 1978) – things are now seen as being 'for real'. Occupation, lifestyle, friendships and relationships may all seem to be 'settling down', with young adults glimpsing a plateau ahead that is reminiscent of the growth–stability–decline model that, perhaps implicitly and generally erroneously, often informs our assumptions about the nature of the life course. After the turbulence of adolescence and fledgling adulthood, the period of early adulthood may seem more concerned with consolidation and incremental growth – a structure-building phase in the language of Daniel Levinson – and less demanding of the need for counselling. The losses of this life stage – loss of youthful freedom from responsibilities and loss of such entwined relationships with parents and siblings – may pass unrecognised by the young people themselves, by their families, by friends and even by therapists (Walsh and McGoldrick, 1988).

Normative pressures to establish an independent 'adult' lifestyle may encourage a denial of the importance of continued relationships with one's family of origin. Because leaving home is regarded as a ritual proof of achieving adult autonomy, we may underestimate the significance of what is lost. Young adults themselves may question and doubt any continuing attachments – accepting the dictum that by now they should have untied themselves from the apron strings of their childhood home. There is, however, evidence (Troll, 1989) that young adults typically keep in close contact with their parents, although this does not mean that things remain the same. Intergenerational relationships within the family must shift from an adult–child relationship involving dependency and control, towards a more equal relationship between adults. It is especially in families where relationships have been particularly close or characterised by intense conflict, that fear of sliding back into a previous dependency may lead young adults to sever, at least temporarily, all links with their family of origin. However, generally a state of 'intimacy at a distance' (Troll, 1989) is ultimately attained. Whilst not many young adults live together with their parents, many do live fairly close and will visit frequently. If the distances are too great, then they will generally talk regularly on the phone, and undertake longer visits at less frequent intervals.

The paucity of attention given to the counselling needs of young adults may stem in part from erroneous assumptions about the nature of this life stage, but also from the fact that no longer are large numbers of the age group sharing similar educational experiences, as has been the case from entry into primary school until graduation from higher education. Members of this age group are more widely dispersed across different institutions than has been the case in their lives hitherto. Lifestyles are becoming increasingly diverse. However, the boundaries between different life stages are blurred and overlapping, and the problems associated with employment, relationships and money that were identified as characteristic of fledgling adulthood may persist into this life stage. In addition, young adults may find themselves:

- reluctant and hesitant to take on the responsibilities of adult life – wondering, perhaps, if they want to – or are capable of – really 'standing on their own two feet';

■ experiencing anxiety and uncertainty over child-bearing decisions, or difficulties in relation to child-rearing – including problems of raising children as lone parents.

In previous generations, and especially for women, the prospect of reaching the age of 30 often signalled an increase in awareness of the ticking of the 'biological clock'. Twenty years ago, young women frequently wished, and believed it was necessary, either to have had their first child by the time they were 30, or, at least, to have clear plans about whether and when they would do so (Sugarman, 1985). However, demographics change, and the birth rate among women in their 20s continues to fall (Stationery Office, 2001). It is predicted that the birth rate among women aged 25–29 years will soon be lower than the birth rate among women aged 30–33, meaning that the age 30 transition has largely lost its significance as a 'last chance saloon' for motherhood. Nonetheless, miscarriage, stillbirth, abortion and infertility are losses that affect a significant number of women and couples, and issues around fertility and the transition to parenthood can be highly emotive concerns of clients at this stage. By the end of their 30s, however, most young adults who are to become parents will have done so. A developmental task for this decade is frequently, therefore, the adjustment to parenthood; or, for those who, whether out of choice or not, do not become parents, managing the consequences of deviating from this social norm.

With the arrival of children, parents' developmental tasks become yoked to those of their children, and the couple relationship has to be renegotiated. Parenthood frequently exacerbates the difficulties of achieving a satisfactory work–home balance. Former leisure activities may be squeezed out, and friendships, particularly with friends who do not themselves have children, may fall by the wayside. Stereotyping, and what Huyuk and Guttman (1999) describe as the 'parental emergency' of the child-rearing years, may increase pressure for couples to adopt role specialisation during the woman's 'window of fertility'. It is still mothers who overwhelmingly assume greater responsibility than fathers for childcare. Therapists may find themselves working with clients to help them prioritise roles, activities and relationships, and to find ways of responding to multiple, pressing demands. For some, coming to terms with 'non-events' may be an issue – the career path that did not materialise or proved disappointing; the stable relationship that did not develop or did not last; the baby that was not conceived. In each case, assumptions, expectations and hopes – largely socially constructed – may be dashed.

Counselling with people in middle adulthood

For most clients, middle adulthood is a time of multiple and some-times conflicting roles, demands and opportunities, making the resources a person has available for dealing with this complexity one of the key therapeutic issues of this life stage (Biggs, 2003). There have, historically, been several different interpretations of midlife (Hunter and Sundel, 1989; Biggs, 1999): as a *plateau* – with, for example, mid-career being seen as a time of 'maintenance'; as an over-whelming *crisis*, whereby a person's coping resources are severely stretched; as a period of challenging change and *transition*, although not necessarily crisis; and as a period of *continuity* involving more incremental than dramatic change. Furthermore, midlife may be presented either in positive fashion as 'the peak period of life', where people are 'wise and powerful – in charge of themselves and others', or, more negatively, as the herald of 'a downhill slide in energy, attractiveness, occupational performance, and happiness at home' (Hunter and Sundel, 1989: 13). These different interpretations will influence, perhaps unknowingly, both clients' and therapists' expectations about midlife and this may lead to difficulties in the therapeutic situation (Biggs, 2003). Seeing midlife issues as depressing and without solution may lead therapists to resist confronting issues of ageing (Woolfe and Biggs, 1997). Seeing age as irrelevant – being 'age blind' – may create false expectations of what is possible, ignoring the need for developing resilience to the inevitable losses that accompany passage through the life course and the need to adapt to forms of decline (Heckhausen, 2001). Seeing midlife as inevitably a time of crisis may result in an exaggeration of the significance of everyday issues and problems, or – by way of contrast – ignoring them as intractable and unavoidable.

Life adjustment problems that clients in middle adulthood may typically bring to counselling coalesce around concerns regarding work and career, family commitments and health (including sexual potency). Specific concerns include (Thomas, 1990):

- the need to change career or to retire, either because skills no longer fit the needs of a changing job market, or because the ability to cope with the demands of the job has diminished with age;
- stress at work, and the desire to resolve job dissatisfaction and/or conflict between job responsibilities, family commitments and diminishing energies;
- the need to renegotiate relationships with partner, with children (as they move towards and achieve independent adulthood) and

with parents (who may be becoming increasingly dependent, vulnerable and demanding);

- the wish to find meaningful occupation and purpose, either within or beyond the workplace, as children grow up and leave home;
- concern about the physical changes often associated with midlife in terms of physical appearance, diminishing sexual desire and potency, and, for women, the approach, occurrence and implication of the menopause;
- grief following the death of a child, parent, partner or close friend.

These issues are often interrelated, rarely arising in isolation. Thus, middle adulthood is the life stage during which demands of both career and family may be at their peak. In the family arena, midlife often coincides with children's long passage from adolescence to adulthood. Not only does this serve as a reminder to the midlife adult of their own ageing, but also requires that the parent, as well as the child, is involved in the renegotiation of relationships that characterises this transition. Powerful feelings around autonomy and encroaching dependency may arise (Biggs, 2003). Furthermore, once children have left home, parents can no longer use their children to mask problems in their relationship with each other (King, 1980). Seeing offspring successfully take on the mantle of adulthood may lead parents to reflect on, and perhaps regret, the choices they have made in their own lives (Cooper, 2003). At work, the increasingly apparent presence and advancement of 'the younger generation' serves as another reminder of the passage of time.

As a result of increasing life expectancy, midlife adults may also find themselves implicated in the transitions of their parents through late adulthood. As children become more independent, so parents may become more dependent and needy. For much of middle adulthood the midlifer may be part of a 'sandwich' generation – caught, it might sometimes feel, between the demands and needs of both those ahead and those following on behind in the human race.

Whilst there are clear and observable physiological changes in both men and women during the middle years (Weg, 1989), it is the awareness and perception of these changes that is of prime importance. Thus, the menopause is a socially constructed as well as a physiological transition (Dan and Bernhard, 1989) that, in contrast to its image as crisis, leaves many women feeling freer, more in control of their lives and enjoying improved communication (including sexual). However, health problems – or at least the possibility of them – may become more apparent during middle adulthood, exacerbated by the illness or death of contemporaries. This can lead (Neugarten, 1968) to an increased sense of physical vulnerability in men and preparations for widowhood in women, leading to a restructuring of life in terms of 'time left to live' rather than 'time since birth'. The awareness of mortality that this denotes is seen as the basis of the apocryphal midlife crisis (Jaques, 1965, 1980).

Counselling with older adults

Whilst all counsellors will have experienced young, and possibly middle, adulthood, few will have had 'first-hand' (Scrutton, 1989) experience of late adulthood. This brings the advantage that clients can be faced without interference from the counsellor's direct experience of this life stage, but increases the scope for counsellors to fall foul of unsubstantiated stereotypes and unarticulated assumptions concerning later life. Older clients are underrepresented in the case loads of many counsellors (Richards, 2001; Goudie, 2003), and older people themselves, the counsellors who might serve them and the cultural conditions within which counselling operates all contribute to the relative absence of older clients from counselling services other than those specifically targeted at their needs.

Ageism can – as was discussed in Chapter 1 – be directed at all age groups, but it is older people who experience it most pervasively and acutely, with late adulthood frequently being portrayed as inevitably a period of deficit, decline and disease. Oldageism can be seen (Butler, 1969) as reflecting 'a deep-seated uneasiness on the part of the young and middle-aged – a personal revulsion to and distaste for growing old, disease, disability; and a fear of powerlessness, "uselessness", and death' (p. 243). Alternatively, and in contradiction to this, there may be a denial that late adulthood does or should in any way differ from midlife. Fear of death is perhaps the major factor underlying oldageism, and a significant component of counsellors' reluctance to work with older clients.

Themes that emerge in work with older clients frequently revolve around loss (Thomas, 1990; O'Leary, 1996). Whilst the passage through all life stages involves entanglement with both gain and loss, in later life the balance between them shifts from the former to the latter (Heckhausen and Lang, 1996). These losses can occur in many areas of clients' lives, and include (Thomas, 1990; Twining, 1996):

- loss of significant friends and partner, either through death, or through loss of contact, with the consequent loss of love and companionship;
- loss of a meaningful parental role, with the possibility of role reversal, whereby children (themselves in midlife) adopt the role of carers for their parents;
- loss of health and strength and/or cognitive decline, with the consequent loss of independence;
- loss of occupational identity or other role denoting contribution to wider society.

Older people may lack knowledge about the availability of counselling services or else, because of generational and cultural factors, may not see the relevance of such services to their own condition (Goudie, 2003). They may have a negative image of therapy, seeing it as shameful or indicative of weakness (Twining, 1996). Counsellors, living within a culture characterised by greater acceptance of and support for counselling, need to be wary of pathologising older people's reluctance to disclose their life stories in counselling. Older people may imbibe prevailing ageist attitudes and believe that they and their problems are not worth the counsellor's time. They may fear the dependency that receiving counselling may indicate and engender (Woolfe, 1998). Transference issues may be different with older clients (King, 1980; Knight, 1996). Rather than, or as well as, the more usual parental transference, older (and, indeed, some midlife) clients may encounter the therapist as representing their children or even their grandchildren. They may question whether, given their lack of experience of old age, 'young' counsellors can empathise or understand what they are going through.

As is the case with children, older people may lack both the economic and social power necessary to access services of which they are aware, including counselling (Pilgrim, 1997). The social consequences of loss of functioning in older people may trigger concern in others, who then refer the older person to services. This influences which problems are addressed. Although depression is twice as prevalent amongst older adults as is dementia, because of the chaos and dangers created by the loss of cognitive functioning, it is dementia that tends to be given greater attention as a mental health problem (Pilgrim, 1997). Not only does this reduce the likelihood of clients' real needs being addressed, but also reinforces the stereotype of late adulthood as a period of cognitive decline. Thus, like children, older people frequently receive mental health services not because they themselves have asked for them, but because of the problems they cause for third parties who have the power to define (and control) problematic behaviour and experience.

When counsellors do work with older clients, countertransference issues may be prevalent (Sprung, 1989; Knight, 1996). Clients in late adulthood bring with them the reminder *memento mori* – remember you will die – thereby forcing counsellors to face their own ageing; its inevitability, and the risks and fears it brings of disability and dependency (Twining, 1996). Older clients may also remind counsellors of their own parents or grandparents, leading to distortions of clinical judgement (Knight, 1996). Nonetheless, death from natural causes is more common amongst older than younger clients, and so counsellors working with those in late adulthood need to be prepared for the death of a client. Whilst they may be afraid of dying, many older people have confronted their own mortality and are not afraid of death. Indeed, in the face of serious ill health or disability they may express the view that they think they would be better off dead. Whilst talk of wanting to die must be taken seriously, it is not necessarily a sign of depression (Twining, 1996).

Counsellors may feel unequal to the task of working with older clients. It might seem arrogant to presume to be able to help someone who has been through life stages the counsellor has only glimpsed at (Richards, 2001). Nonetheless, there may also be fear that the older client's demands could be overwhelming and endless (Martindale, 1989). To avoid working with older clients and to separate them off as 'different from me' is to gain some protection, at least temporarily, from the fears that working with them might provoke. This may, however, generate feelings of guilt about what one is doing, and also about one's own privilege, health and vigour in comparison to frail and vulnerable clients in late adulthood (Viney, 1993).

Whilst most older people function well, both physically and cognitively, through into their 70s or 80s, the counsellor working with older clients does need to be aware of factors that may impede communication (Scrutton, 1989; Twining, 1996). Poor hearing may impair the ability to hold a therapeutic conversation. Poor eyesight may restrict the opportunities for non-verbal communication. Ill health or frailty may impose limits on the length and location of sessions. However, it is important to remember that these restrictions exist because of the client's impairments, not *per se* because of his or her age.

Parallels as well as distinctions

The present chapter has focused on the dissimilarities of different life stages. However, whilst each life stage is *distinctive*, it is also true that life stages are not *distinct* in the sense of being separate and isolated. Whilst it is important, when working with any age group, to be aware of their particular qualities and vulnerabilities, it is equally important to be aware of the connection between different life stages. Although people of different ages differ, their concerns and preoccupations are not as different as perhaps they might appear. There are wide-ranging and fundamental psychological themes that may appear in varying forms at any phase of life. These include (Brown and Smith, 1996) attachment, loss, separation, hope, fear, anger, hostility and love. Many writers focusing on clients of a particular age or life stage reiterate this point. Thus, Mabey and Sorensen (1995), writing about adolescence, comment on the similarities between this transition and the process of individuation that happens in early childhood, during which the child learns to see him- or herself as a person separate from, and yet dependent on, the primary care provider:

> Just as the successful conclusion of this early process in human development is dependent on a mother's willingness to allow a child to move out of the symbiotic relationship towards individuation, so in adolescence a successful conclusion of the process requires a parent or carer to recognize, allow and facilitate a young person's need to move out of the dependent role of child in the family towards independence, autonomy and maturity. (p. 7)

There is interplay and interaction between the concerns and developmental tasks characteristic of different life stages. For example, the social network of parents with young children frequently comprises the parents of other children of a similar age to their own – irrespective of the age of the parents. Thus, the 20-year-old parent of a toddler and the 45-year-old parent of a toddler may see themselves at a broadly similar life stage – even though, by the framework adopted in the present chapter, they would have been identified as being in fledgling adulthood and middle adulthood, respectively. Another example is the interplay between the developmental preoccupations of adolescents and their parents. It is often the timing of the departure of adolescents or fledgling adults from their childhood home that determines to a significant extent when parents re-evaluate their own future and confront issues in their relationship that have been masked by child-rearing responsibilities.

Whilst being of different ages, life stages and generations sometimes separates and distinguishes us, our position on this dimension of difference is continually changing. Although we may choose not to dwell on it, we either were or can anticipate reaching the age and life stage of those many years our junior or senior. This points to a key distinction between ageism, on the one hand, and sexism and racism on the other (Andrews, 1999). Although sex change and skin pigmentation operations do exist, for most people the categories of sex and race are constants. Our age classification, however, is not static. Whilst people who behave in a racist or sexist manner are unlikely ever to be members of the group that is the target of their discrimination, ageism is unique in that those who practise it were once a member of, or will one day join (if longevity is granted them), the group they presently discriminate against. Ageism identifies those of different ages as 'the other', and creates an artificial 'them' and 'us' divide between different life stages.

4

Transitions and turning points

'Things end, there is a time of fertile emptiness, and then things begin anew'.

(William Bridges, 1980)

Counsellors often become implicated – possibly as key actors – in the turning points of clients' lives. Indeed, counselling services may be organised around key life events or transitions – career decisions, bereavement, abortion, for example. A focus on transitions draws us into what has been termed 'the fulcrum of the change process' (Nicholson and West, 1988: 2). Some of these transitions may be associated with a particular life stage, another organising principle for many counselling services.

But what exactly is a transition? Whilst a number of definitions jostle for consideration, it is useful from both a life course and a counselling perspective, to think of transitions as occurring if an event or non-event triggers changes in the assumptions people hold about themselves and the world, leading – in most cases – to a corresponding change in behaviour and interpersonal relationships (Schlossberg, 1981; Schlossberg et al., 1995). From a life course perspective, a key point of note in this definition is the inclusion of non-events as well as events as triggers of transitions. Assuming the existence of a social time clock whereby we, perhaps implicitly, assume our life will pan out in certain ways, with particular events – be it getting married, buying a house, taking up full-time employment etc. – occurring (roughly speaking) in a particular order and at particular points in the life course, then, when these events fail to occur as expected we can be propelled into a period of reflection and upheaval as great as if some cataclysmic event had unexpectedly turned our world upside down. Thus, whilst the birth of a first child is undoubtedly a significant life event for virtually all parents (and, indeed, all babies), so too can the failure to conceive trigger – albeit more gradually – the change in self-perception and interpretation that is the hallmark of a transition. Whilst all turning points are transitions, not all transitions are necessarily turning points – transitions may still leave a person on the same life trajectory as before, whilst turning points mark a redirection of the course of a person's life (Rutter, 1996) and/or a significant change in self-understanding (McAdams, 1997).

From a counselling perspective, another notable feature of this definition of a transition is the attention it gives to the experience and understandings of the person undergoing the transition. It recognises that transitions can be states of mind as well as external events (Bridges, 1980), and it prioritises the internal state of mind and the meaning of an event to the individual over any external manifestations of change. Try to take time out at this point to complete Activity 8: Transitions and turning points, so that your own experience can inform your consideration of the discussion of transitions that follows.

Activity 8: Transitions and turning points

Think back over your life and list its major landmarks – the events and experiences that stand out as significant in some way. Go for quantity – say between 12 and 25 events. Make your initial list, then think again – 'Is there anything else that I have left out?'

- Place the letter 'T' alongside those of the above experiences that marked a turning point in your life.
- Select two of these turning points to look at in more detail and, for each of them, consider the following questions:
  - What made this a turning point?
  - Did I realise at the time that it was a turning point?
  - What difficulties did it cause me?
  - Did anything or anybody help? If so, in what ways?
  - How and when did I know the turning point was over?
  - How was I different afterwards from before?

■ Now return to your list of events, and consider:
  − What *types* of event did I include in my original list?
  − *When* did most of these events typically occur? Were they evenly spaced through the life course, or did they bunch together at particular points?

Whilst much can be learned from reflecting on these questions on your own, even more can be gained if you have the opportunity to compare and discuss your responses with a few other people who have also completed the exercise.

Whereas most approaches to the life course provide a 'broad sweep' across time via stages or themes, a transitional approach, in focusing on turning points and particular developmental tasks, has a more narrow perspective. It looks at life events − significant markers within the life course that clients might well bring to counselling − as dynamic experiences having 'antecedents, durations, contexts and outcomes' (Reese and Smyer, 1983: 2). Placing these experiences in a life course context emphasises how the new 'post-transition' life is always built on the identity that went before. Some parts of the previous self remain. This contributes to the uniqueness of each client and, indeed, counsellor. Two counsellors, no matter how similar their training, will always be very different counsellors, each having what Schlossberg et al. (1995) refer to as a 'hang-over identity'.

The transitional perspective is, therefore, another 'take' on the life course that counsellors might usefully be aware of. You probably already have a good understanding of the commonly occurring transitions in the client group with which you generally work − be this transitions into or out of employment, geographic relocation, leaving home, having a child, coming out as lesbian or gay. The present chapter strives to place this knowledge in a wider, more general framework that provides a way of connecting our understanding of events in different domains and across different stages in the life course.

Transition sequences

Elisabeth Kubler-Ross's (1970) work on death and dying has provided one of the most influential and widely disseminated models of transition. It is a landmark example of a life event being viewed as a long-term process rather than a point-in-time occurrence. The model proposes five distinct, but overlapping stages in the process of facing and coming to terms with death. Although distinct, the stages will frequently overlap and are not necessarily progressive in that not everyone will proceed through them all. The five stages are:

- *denial* – the refusal to believe a terminal diagnosis;
- *anger* – often directed at family members or medical staff;
- *bargaining* – negotiating with God or some other higher being for more time;
- *depression* – beginning to acknowledge and mourn the impending loss;
- *acceptance* – acquiescing to and no longer fighting the inevitable.

This formulation has had an immense impact on the attitude and practice of professionals working with the dying, and has been widely popularised in books for those facing terminal illness and their families. However, it is important to look at the experience of facing death in a life course context. Kubler-Ross's model was based on studies carried out with people in young and middle adulthood who were dying of cancer. The timing of their death cut short the normally expected life span, and this could be a basis for both the denial and the anger. Amongst older people who have already lived longer than they expected to, acceptance without denial may be easier. Also, the fact that cancer can go into and out of remission may make denial seem a more rational response and provide a justification for bargaining rather than resignation to the inevitable. In other words, the timing, the nature of the illness and the individual's interpretation of the situation are all important.

Kubler-Ross's 'phases of dying' bear a close resemblance to John Bowlby's (1980) 'phases of grief': shock or numbness; pining, yearning and protest; disorganisation and despair; and readjustment. Bowlby's first phase includes the urge to deny the truth of the loss, his second phase includes anger, his third is characterised by feelings of depression, and his final phase involves some sort of reconciliation to or acceptance of the new situation. Many other losses have been studied (see, for example, Murgatroyd and Woolfe, 1982; Fisher and Cooper, 1990), and in the mid-1970s a generalised model of transition dynamics was proposed (Hopson and Adams, 1976; Hopson, 1981), suggesting that disruptions to our accustomed way of life trigger a relatively predictable cycle of reactions and feelings. Although the model is a general pattern rather than a rigid sequence, and despite significant individual differences, the cycle is sufficiently generalisable for most people to relate its seven stages to their own experience of at least some major life events. The stages in this wave of emotions are as follows.

- *Immobilisation* – shock, being unable to comprehend what has happened, being overwhelmed by the situation, and being 'frozen in one's tracks'. This stage is characterised by a sense of disbelief – 'This can't really be happening' – and inability to make plans.
- *Reaction and minimisation* – an emotional swing, either positive or negative, depending on the nature of the transition, that breaks through the shock and includes a tendency to minimise, trivialise or even deny the change.
- *Self-doubt* – a period of uncertainty and, as the demands of the transition become apparent, a sense of powerlessness. Often accompanied by feelings of depression, this stage may also include feelings of anxiety or sadness and fluctuations between anger and apathy.
- *Acceptance of reality and letting go* – a gradual realisation that the fact of the transition cannot be undone, and the beginning of a reorientation from the past towards the future.
- *Testing* – a time of trying out new options and actively experimenting with new behaviours or lifestyles. Whilst there may be rapid mood swings as plans are considered and rapidly discarded, overall, both mood and energy level generally improve.
- *Search for meaning* – a conscious striving to make sense of what has happened, learn from the experience and understand the meaning of the transition. Whilst still infused with emotion, this stage has a stronger cognitive element – it is as if the balance tips towards thinking rather than feeling.
- *Integration* – finding a place for the transition in the wider life course context so that it becomes an integral part of who one is; an integration, in other words, of new and old elements of the life structure.

Although not explicitly incorporated into the Activity Trail (I decided that a round dozen of exercises was the maximum I should include), it can be instructive to examine one or two of your own transitions and see to what extent you can identify these stages. To what extent did your experience conform to the sequence described above? Which were the most and which the least distinguishable of the stages? How long did each stage last? When you moved on, did you leave the previous stage once and for all, or did you return to it on more than one occasion? It is possible to divine this sequence in the most trivial of decisions – the five-minute dilemma, for example, of what to do when the film we had planned to see is not being screened: do we go out for a meal instead, or go to see a different film? However, if the above sequence makes the process sound simple or straightforward whatever the transition, then nothing could be farther from the truth. For significant life events the process can extend over several years, and may indeed be a lifelong undertaking that never reaches completion.

Stage theories of transition have been both widely accepted and widely criticised. A main and general criticism centres around rejection of what is seen as the 'one-size-fits-all' mentality of the transition cycle. The sequence of stages is seen as a denial of individual differences and an attempt to force people's experience into preordained categories rather than work with the unique experience of a unique individual. As with critiques of life stage theories, this is partly the result of oversimplifying and caricaturing the stage models. Hopson and Adams' (1976) model, for example, comes laden with many caveats.

- Passage through the cycle is rarely smooth and one-directional. People vacillate between stages and may be working on several stages simultaneously. This is consistent with the dual process model that distinguishes two different aspects of grief (Stroebe and Stroebe, 1987; Stroebe et al., 1992). One aspect is loss oriented, and consists of facing grief, breaking the ties and renegotiating the bonds with the deceased; and the other is restoration oriented, and involves activities that distance the bereaved from the situation in an attempt to return to 'normal' life (denial and suppression of the grief, avoidance of the subject, doing other things as a distraction from the grief). It is argued that, in order to cope fully with grief we need to oscillate and obtain some sort of balance between the two types of activity – which, incidentally, can be seen as reflecting, respectively, the 'fight' and 'flight' aspects of the stress response (Cannon, 1939). This, in turn, can be seen as a vacillation between the earlier and later stages of Hopson's model.
- There is no 'correct' or 'typical' duration for any stage. This will vary depending on the individual and the particular transition. For bereavements and other significant losses, the duration is likely to be years rather than weeks, or even months.

- It is not assumed that all individuals will complete the cycle with regard to every transition. We may become 'stuck' at any stage. We may not want to move on, or we may not know how to. It could be that we become distracted as other events and demands compete for our attention – transitions will often bunch together rather than occur neatly one after the other.
- There is great variation across individuals and situations in the magnitude of the response to transition. It can range from a virtually imperceptible ripple to a breathtaking roller-coaster of extreme emotions.

In sum, any particular transition must be considered in the context of the particular individual, the particular transition, and the particular social and personal circumstances – including life stage. Nonetheless, and despite all of the above caveats and qualifications, the transition cycle offers signposts as to how the emotional concomitants to change – and in particular loss – are likely to pan out for the individual. Whilst each person's experience of loss is unique, this does not mean it shares nothing with any other experience – either the experiences of other people or other experiences of the same person. In the same way as age norms can provide guidance and a degree of predictability as well as a set of constraining obligations and expectations, so, too, can knowledge of the transition cycle be a guide rather than a strait-jacket – providing hope, a sense of direction and reassurance that things need not always remain the same. Recognising that the sequence of emotions described in the transition cycle is 'normal' (that is, not inherently pathological) and 'normative' (that is, experienced by others as well as ourselves) can be reassuring, helping to rescue us from the loneliness of our suffering.

The transition cycle serves to suggest how clients' needs may change during the course of counselling as they move between different stages of the cycle. Although the stages in the transition sequence are generally discussed in relation to changing levels of self-esteem or mood, the model does incorporate both emotional and cognitive elements. In the first part of the cycle the focus is primarily emotional, with the increasing involvement of the cognitive process as the person moves through the Testing and Search for meaning stages. Arguably, the focus of counselling should similarly change as a client moves through these stages.

Accepting reality and letting go

Whilst all stages in the transition sequence could be discussed at great length, it is the fourth stage – that of accepting reality and letting go – that warrants particular comment. It is both the middle stage in the sequence and a watershed in the transition process. Often occurring around an emotional low point, the stage of Accepting reality and letting go marks the point at which the past starts to relinquish its hold on the present, thereby allowing the person to begin moving forward and looking to the future. 'Letting go' need not, however, involve the total severance of links. It is not that we 'put the past behind us' and leave it there. More usually, ties are loosened and renegotiated, rather than broken completely.

This interpretation of letting go as a loosening rather than a severance of ties, is consistent with current theorising about the process of coping with loss – in particular bereavement. Traditionally, at least in twentieth-century Western societies, disengagement from the past has been seen as the mark of successful grief resolution, with continued attachment to the deceased being interpreted as symptomatic of psychological problems. More recently, however (see, for example, Klass et al., 1996; Walter, 1999; Neimeyer, 2001), attention has turned to the ways in which a dead person 'is lost and then refound, rather than clung onto before being ultimately relinquished' (Walter, 1996: 9). Rather than being expunged from a person's current narrative, the deceased is integrated into a durable biography that has meaning for the bereaved in the present. Thus, Worden (1995) amended the fourth of his well-known list of the tasks of mourning and grief counselling. The first three remained: to accept the reality of the loss; to work through the pain of grief; and to adjust to an environment in which the deceased is missing. The fourth task was recast as the need to emotionally relocate the deceased and move on with life (amended from the earlier version (Worden, 1983) – withdrawing emotional energy from the deceased and reinvesting it in another relationship).

It has increasingly been recognised that ties to the past are not renounced, but are reformulated as we reconstruct our personal biography. This process applies to other occasions when our world is turned upside down, not only to bereavement and mourning. Physical separation from another person, place or role, even if permanent, does not mean that we must inevitably move on without them, but rather that we work to 'find a secure place' for them in our present life (Walter, 1996). This thread of continuing rather than (or as well as) breaking bonds during transition links together a person's experience across the life course into a more coherent whole. It reflects the theme of continuity within change.

Nonetheless, letting go inevitably involves a plunge into the unknown. Even if links with the past are maintained, much does change. Bridges' concept of embracing the opportunities of the 'neutral' zone (the 'time of fertile emptiness' in this chapter's epigraph) existing between the old past and the new future offers a way of exploiting the opportunities offered by being betwixt and between. It involves giving time and space to a formless and fallow period, out of which new beginnings should not be forced, but instead allowed to emerge – often indirectly and unimpressively. The temptation may be to rush through the void, or else stay tied to the former life structure, and it is here that counselling may have a crucial role to play.

Fertile emptiness

The neutral zone is a state of loss and emptiness between an ending and a new beginning, and, as such, can be disconcerting. There is nothing to hold us steady, we do not know where we are and there is nothing to aim for. And yet the emptiness of the neutral zone is more than the absence of something. It is 'a moratorium from the conventional activity of our everyday existence' (Bridges, 1980: 114) that allows for personal reflection, reappraisal and redirection. However, instead of welcoming and making constructive use of the neutral zone, when we experience endings we frequently try to replace the missing elements as quickly as possible. Whilst instruction and ritual, argues Bridges, helped the members of traditional societies through the wilderness of the neutral zone, today we must 'fashion our own tools' (p. 117) – specifically learning how to *surrender* ourself to the emptiness of the neutral zone, and then *amplify* its intensity so as to exploit the opportunities for self-renewal that it contains.

■ *Surrender* involves giving in to the emptiness and chaos of nothingness, and not struggling to escape – thereby allowing for inner reorientation. 'The transition process involves an inner realignment and a renewal of energy, both of which depend on immersion in the chaos of the neutral zone' (p. 136). The temptation may be to rush through the neutral zone, but this is to miss the opportunity of using this time 'between dreams' (p. 112) as a place within which 'a new sense of self could gestate' (p. 112).

- To *amplify* the neutral zone experience is to make it more real and vivid, thereby encouraging the discovery of meaning in amongst the chaos: 'Chaos is not a mess, but rather it is the primal state of pure energy to which the person returns for every true new beginning. It is only from the perspective of the old form that chaos looks fearful – from any other perspective it looks like life itself' (pp. 119–20). In order to encourage the emergence and appreciation of opportunities for self-renewal afforded by the neutral zone, Bridges suggests several ways of amplifying the neutral zone experience (see Box 4.1). Ironically, such strategies are likely to hasten the passage through this zone and on to a new beginning.

Box 4.1: Making the most of being betwixt and between

William Bridges (1980) argues that during transitions we must, at least to some extent, lose our current identity before we are free to create it anew. This creates a gap – or 'neutral zone' – between the ending and the new beginning. He further argues that modern society has lost the capacity to value and make constructive use of the emptiness and confusion of the neutral zone. He suggests strategies to help us resist the temptation to rush through or refuse to enter the neutral zone and, instead, to exploit the opportunities it provides for redirection and renewal. Strategies include:

- *Finding a regular time and place to be quietly alone.*
- *Beginning a journal of earlier neutral-zone experiences.* What was going on? What was your mood? What were you thinking about, perhaps without realising it, at the time? What puzzling or unusual things happened? What decisions do you wish you could have made? What dreams do you remember having?.
- *Writing an autobiography.* When something ends – a relationship, a course of study, a holiday – we have a natural tendency to look back over it and reminisce. This helps us put the experience in some sort of order, reinterpret it and attain closure (at least for the moment). Writing an autobiography helps us to discover similarities between seemingly different experiences, and to bring to conscious awareness insights that we might otherwise but dimly appreciate. (See, also, Activity 3: Life chapters, and Activity 11: Exploring your story – other ways of encouraging the writing of our life story.)
- *Thinking of what would be unlived in your life if it ended today.* From your vantage point in the emptiness of the neutral zone, reflect on your thoughts and feelings about the past: 'What was unlived in that past – what

dreams, what convictions, what talents, what ideas, what qualities went unrealized?' (p. 126). Use the neutral zone as an opportunity to redirect your life, to do something different, to begin a new chapter.

- *Taking a neutral-zone retreat.* Cultivate receptivity to whatever emerges from your thoughts and feelings by spending a few days in an unfamiliar place, free of distractions and normal day-to-day demands in order to reflect consciously on the transition process that is enveloping you.

Stability zones and convoys

Daniel Levinson (Levinson et al., 1978) called on a nautical metaphor to describe the transitional experience. It is like being adrift on a raft in the open sea – cast off from the past, but with the land of the future not yet in view. The risk, and the fear, is that we may go astray – assuming we even know where it is we are heading. However, whilst the focus in considering transitions is primarily on movement and change, it is valuable to look also at the counterbalance to this – those things that might hold us steady, offering some sort of mooring or anchor (to continue the nautical analogy). Toffler (1970) suggests that we can cope with large amounts of complexity and confusion provided at least one area of our life is relatively stable. Such stability zones are typically associated (Pedler et al., 2001) with people, ideas, places, things, and organisations.

- *People* stability zones are sources of social support. They provide the benefits of enduring relationships, and may include family, friends and colleagues. Counsellors' supervisory relationships may often be experienced in this light. Of particular relevance in the present context is the issue of the extent to which counsellors can, do and should represent stability zones for their clients.
- *Ideas* that are stability zones are tenets of belief. These may include deeply felt religious convictions, or a strong personal and/or professional commitment to a philosophy, political ideology or cause. For counsellors, their theoretical orientation can provide a stability zone. Skovholt and Ronnestad (1995) noted the strong identification, possibly the over-identification, of trainee counsellors with the theoretical approach in which they were being trained. It provides 'something to hang onto', some sort of guiding light in an otherwise unfathomable world.

- *Places* of varying proportions can comprise stability zones. They might be large scale (like a country) or small scale (for example, a street or a particular room). 'Home' is often a stability zone, a place with a comforting familiarity about it, perhaps where one grew up or has spent considerable time.
- *Things* as stability zones take the form of favourite, familiar, comforting possessions. They might range from family heirlooms, through particular objects to favourite items of clothes. Keeping a memento of someone who has died acknowledges the role of things as stability zones by both providing a link to our past and helping to secure a place for the deceased person in our current life structure.
- *Organisations* that operate as stability zones may be our employer, a professional body, a social club, or any other organisation to which one belongs and with which one identifies. For clients, the appeal of self-help organisations is frequently that they offer support to people seeking to connect with others 'in the same boat', thereby reducing loneliness and confusion (Killilea, 1976; Stewart, 1990; Kurtz, 1997). Jacobs (2000) plots and discusses the enormous growth in number and membership of associations for therapists. Such associations can provide professional, intellectual, social and emotional stability zones.

Stability zones may overlap – 'home' has elements of place, people and things, for example; 'books' have elements of things and ideas; and 'the workplace' may have elements of all stability zones. Whilst counselling often concentrates on change, the clarification and nurturing of stability zones – for self as well as for clients – can be a useful counterbalance to this, and is addressed in the second Activity Trail exercise for this chapter, Activity 9: Stability zones.

Activity 9: Stability zones

Some people find it very important to experience the continuities in their lives when so much else is changing. I am typing these words right now on our dining room table, for example, a table that my parents bought before I was born, a table that I ate all my childhood meals on, a table that represents to me the whole New England world that is my background. And now, living in California, raising my children differently from the way I was raised, directing my life toward goals that are very different from those with which I started, I find real pleasure in the fact that this important new beginning of mine is being written on something that is old and dear to me.

(Bridges, 1980)

On this occasion the Activity Trail exercise begins with an invitation to reflect on an aspect of your counselling practice. Think about two or three clients you have worked with and use the following questions to reflect on the extent to which the concept of stability zones was a conscious or an implicit factor in your work.

- What were my client's stability zones? How aware was I, at the time, of the stability zones that my client could call upon outside the counselling relationship?
- How *effective* were my client's stability zones? Did they fulfil the role of holding the client steady whilst other aspects of their life were in turmoil?
- How *stable* were these stability zones? Did they change during the course of counselling? To what extent did the client initiate these changes? To what extent were they beyond the client's control?
- To what extent, and in what ways, did the counselling relationship operate as a stability zone for the client? In what ways was this helpful?

Whilst these questions have all been directed at the experience of clients, they are equally relevant to your own life. The questions that follow invite you to examine your own stability zones.

- *What are your stability zones?* Can you identify stability zones in the areas of people, ideas, places, things and organisations? How well do they serve you? Are they too flimsy to hold you steady? Or are they so strong that they weigh you down and hold you back? Perhaps some of the stability zones that you have depended on in the past have changed. It may be that they no longer offer what you need. It may be that they no longer exist.
- *How well will your stability zones serve you in the future?* To what extent will your current stability zones remain stable, and to what extent will they continue to meet your needs?
- *What needs to change?* Think about what changes you might need or want to make to your stability zones. What can you do to implement these changes? How would you like your stability zones to look in, say, 6 or 12 months' time?
- *How can they be maintained?* What do you do, or need to do, to nurture, develop and maintain your stability zones – the relationships, ideas, values, places, possessions and associations that are important to you?

Several of the questions posed in Activity 9 relate to the fact that stability zones alter over time. Sometimes we instigate these transformations, on other occasions they are imposed on us, irrespective of our wishes. Stability zones, somewhat ironically, whilst holding us steady, also change. Stability is not, in other words, synonymous with stasis. This dynamic element in 'people' stability zones is captured in the concept of a social or interpersonal support convoy (Kahn and Antonucci, 1980; Antonucci, 1991) that accompanies a person through their life course. Represented as a series of concentric circles (see Activity 10), the degree of closeness and permanence of convoy members is indicated by their distance from the focal person, who is placed at the centre of the innermost circle. Those in the outer circle represent convoy members whose relationship with the focal person (the client, in the present context) is entirely role dependent, and are therefore vulnerable to change in role.

It can be salutary to recognise that counsellors and other helping professionals are located on the periphery of this series of concentric rings. The relationship may be very important and significant to the client and, indeed to the counsellor, but it is time-bound and role dependent. Boundary and dual role issues arise if the counsellor gravitates towards the centre. However, not all relationships that begin in this outer circle need remain there. People who started out as role-dependent members of our convoy – fellow students, work colleagues or neighbours, for example – may, over time, move towards the centre. They might, indeed, become members of the innermost circle – those people who are very close to us, and with whom our relationship is no longer role dependent. Frequency of contact or geographic proximity may not be a good indicator of membership of this inner circle of support. Siblings or friends who emigrate to the other side of the world, for example, do not necessarily relinquish their place at the centre of our convoy. This is analogous to the concept of continuing rather than breaking bonds during transition. It may be that for some clients their interpersonal support convoy is sparsely populated. Alternatively they may locate members differently from how those people might place themselves. Thus clients who become angry when counsellors move on, or employees who feel abandoned when their boss or work colleagues leave, may be imagining those people are closer to the centre of the circle than is actually the case. The final Activity Trail exercise of this chapter (Activity 10: Interpersonal support convoys) uses this notion of a support convoy as the basis for exploring a client's life structure, and possibly your own.

Activity 10: Interpersonal support convoys

- Think about the social network in which one of your clients is embedded. List those relationships that, as you understand it, provide your client with important sources of interpersonal support. Categories to consider include:

  Partner　　　　　　　　　　　Work colleagues
  Family　　　　　　　　　　　　Neighbours
  Friends　　　　　　　　　　　Professionals

- Place the individuals identified on the diagram below (adapted from Kahn and Antonucci, 1980):

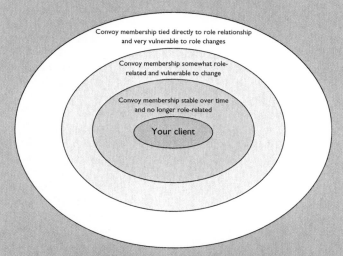

Are there any evident gaps? Are there areas of which you are ignorant? Where is your relationship with the client placed? Does the picture reveal major sources of support beyond the boundaries of the counselling relationship?

- Now think about your own interpersonal support convoy, drawing for yourself a diagram similar to the one above.
- What does your interpersonal support convoy look like? Can you identify people who have moved from the outer to the inner circles? Are there people who have moved in the other direction, possibly leaving the convoy altogether? How well is your interpersonal support convoy serving you? Can you identify areas that you might want to nurture or enhance?

Disruption of our stability zones is, however, not only inevitable, but also desirable. Like Levinson's life structures (of which, indeed they are a part), our stability zones can become outmoded and in need of renewal. Their loss enables us, in the chaos and emptiness of Bridges' neutral zone, to learn in a new sense who we 'really' are. Bridges emphasises how 'the task of finding the significance of a particular transition may be slow and difficult. Unless that significance is found, however, the thread of personal development will be lost' (1980: 78). Finding this significance and integrating it into the client's life story is a prevalent task in counselling. The next chapter explores aspects of this in more detail.

5

Life stories

'*Each of us is a biography, a story. Each of us is a singular narrative, which is constructed, continually, unconsciously, by, through, and in us.*'

(Oliver Sacks, 1985)

Clients present themselves to counsellors through the stories they tell. These stories may, amongst other things, generate a sense of drama, indicate positive potentials, signal future intentions, or invite nurturance and sympathy (Gergen, 1988). Stages, themes, events, transitions, turning points, anchors – the subject matter, in other words, of earlier chapters in this book, are all ways of encompassing, at least in part, the life course that clients reveal during counselling. However, clients rarely bring their life course to counselling neatly packaged in concepts such as these. Rather, clients bring their life course to counselling in the form of a story, a potent metaphor for understanding not only the client's world, but also the counselling process. That their story is in some way problematic or awry is what brings clients into therapy (Howard, 1991). Therapy can then be seen as a process of story repair and (re)construction.

One of the people whose work most completely grounds change and development over the life course in a narrative framework is Dan McAdams (1996, 1997). Before reviewing McAdams' theory, however, Activity 11: Exploring your story uses his interview schedule as a framework for personal reflection. It extends the earlier exercise, Activity 3: Life chapters, and is the most substantial of all the Activity Trail tasks. It is probably best tackled in several chunks rather than all in one go.

Activity 11: Exploring your story

There is not one big cosmic meaning for all, there is only the meaning we each give to our life, an individual meaning, an individual plot, like an individual novel, a book for each person.

(Nin, 1967)

For this exercise, you can work privately, although McAdams recommends working with a 'sympathetic listener' – ideally a friend who has not to date been significant in influencing your life. What follows below is a list of questions that should lead to a reasonably comprehensive account of your personal narrative and also generate information about each of the key story elements identified by McAdams. It is a major undertaking and you may need to be selective in which questions you address. If you are reading this book as part of your training in counselling, the activity might form a focus for some personal development work, or be the basis of a course assignment. Here, only the broad introductory questions are included. More specific questions to address are included in the commentary on the activity in the Appendix. The questions are based on the interview schedule developed by McAdams for his research, the first section of which – *Life chapters* – has already been included as Activity 3 in Chapter 2, as an introduction to the discussion of life stages. The questions below are based on the remaining sections of McAdams' schedule:

(I)   Key events. It may be that you could use here any work that you have done in relation to Activity 8: Transitions and turning points. The task is to reflect on some specific episodes in your past that stand out for some reason and are set in a particular time and place. Examples of key events could be:

- *a peak experience* – a high point in your life story;
- *a nadir experience* – a low point in your life story;
- *a turning point* – an episode where you underwent a significant change in your understanding of yourself;
- *an important early memory* – any memory, either positive or negative, from your childhood that stands out today and that is complete with setting, scene, characters, feelings and thoughts;
- *an important adolescent memory* – any memory, again either positive or negative, from your teenage years that stands out today;
- *an important adult memory* – a memory, positive or negative, that stands out from age 21 onwards.

(II)   Significant people. Now focus on up to *four* of the most important people in your life story and ask yourself these questions.

- What kind of relationship did or do I have with this person?
- What has been their impact on my life story?

(III) **Future script.** Having thought about past events and influences, now consider the future.

- What do I think will happen next in my life story?
- What is my dream for the future?

(IV) **Stresses and problems.** Now consider in detail one or two areas where you are currently experiencing at least one of the following:

- significant stress;
- a major conflict;
- a difficult problem or challenge that must be addressed.

(V) **Personal ideology.** In this section think about your fundamental beliefs and values – your spiritual, political and philosophical position.

(VI) **Overall life theme.** As a finale, look back over your entire life story to see whether you can identify a central theme, message or idea.

Story as identity

When invited to talk about our life course, most of us will tell a story. As authors of our personal narrative, we select from our countless daily experiences what to include in the story and what to omit. We weave what we select into a narrative and link what is happening now with what has passed, and what may happen in the future. 'If we do not exactly write the plots of our lives, nevertheless it is we alone who create our own stories. Agency lies not in governing what shall happen to us, but in creating what we make of what happens. We ourselves construct the meaning of our story' (Salmon, 1985: 138–9). However, the capacity to understand and mould our life in story form emerges only gradually. McAdams' theory of the life course proposes that key structural elements making up a personal narrative develop sequentially and cumulatively across a person's life.

The seeds of our personal narrative are sown, suggests McAdams, during the first year of life, and throughout childhood – even before we consciously know what a story is – we are collecting material for the 'self-defining story we will someday compose' (McAdams, 1997: 13). However, the development of a personal narrative is dependent on the ability to think abstractly – a cognitive achievement attained during adolescence. Accordingly, it is from late adolescence onwards that we begin to use the material and tools acquired thus far to form our life experiences into a coherent, purposeful and meaningful story. Through the adult years we continually refashion our story in an effort to 'articulate a meaningful niche in the psychosocial world' and to provide our life with unity or purpose' (McAdams, 1997: 5). Three of the seven key narrative elements identified by McAdams emerge during infancy and childhood, the fourth towards the end of adolescence, and the remaining three during the years of adulthood:

- *Narrative tone.* McAdams traces the origins of narrative tone – the general sense of optimism or pessimism that pervades a person's narrative – back to the first year of life. The development of secure attachments to primary caregivers leads the infant towards a confident and coherent childhood self, reflected in an optimistic narrative tone that implicitly proclaims the world to be basically trustworthy, predictable, knowable and good. In the face of negative life experiences, an optimistic narrative tone conveys hope for improvement in the future. Insecure attachments, by contrast, lead towards a more pessimistic narrative tone, where it is assumed that wishes and intentions are generally thwarted by a capricious and unpredictable world, so that stories do not have happy endings. Positive events are perceived negatively – as 'too good to be true'.
- *Personal imagery.* Whilst complete stories are too big, complex and ordered for pre-school children to grasp, arresting images – vivid syntheses of feelings, knowledge and inner sensations captured in an episode in time – can serve to make stories memorable. The family is a potent source of such images, both positive and negative. Others derive from wider cultural sources – including language, religion, the media (especially television), stories and customs. Children use these emotionally charged images to help them make sense of their experiences, and whilst many images will be transient, some will survive into adulthood to animate the personal narrative.
- *Motivational themes.* As children progress through formal schooling, their developing cognitive skills enable them to recognise recurrent themes in stories that reflect what the characters want and how they pursue their objectives over time. Appreciation of the motivations and intentions of story characters helps school-age children as they begin to establish their own motivational patterns. Over time, these

patterns become consolidated into stable dispositions that will be reflected thematically in personal narratives.

McAdams identifies two predominant themes in stories that, in turn, reflect two central, and often conflicting, psychological motivations in human lives. One theme is the desire for power – for autonomy and independence; and the other is the desire for love – the wish to relate, merge and surrender the self to another. The delineation of these two fundamental, but contradictory, human motives has itself been a recurrent theme in accounts of human motivation – as in Freud's (1955) counterposing of the 'life instincts' and the 'death instincts' and the frequent reference by (amongst others) Levinson et al. (1978) to the tension between attachment and separation.

- *Ideology*. By adolescence, several key components of the personal narrative are in place. The tendency towards a particular narrative tone has been established, emotionally charged images have been gathered, and motives have been given shape in the themes of power and love. Now a personal ideology – a set of beliefs about what is right and true – is defined. Initial formulations may be simplistic and stereotypical, but, with time, tend to be replaced by more sophisticated and subtle conceptions of what is good and true. The kind of ideological belief system established in adolescence – its structure and its content – will probably stay with us through our adult years, with, in most cases, but minor changes and variations.

Having attained the building blocks of stories we are ready to become a story maker. We become both architect and mason of our own personal narrative.

- *Characters*. Having established the ideological scene in which our personal narrative is to be set, the main story-making task that straddles the stages of fledgling and young adulthood (that is, during the 20s and 30s) concerns the creation and refinement of the story's main characters or imagoes – internalised complexes of actual or imagined people. Life stories may have one dominant character or many, with the existence of two central and often conflicting characters being relatively common. Generally these characters are fashioned around the themes of agency and communion, and whilst it is possible to identify general 'types' of imago there is also great variation and individuality.

- *Generative denouement*. The fashioning and refinement of the characters that people our life stories continues into the years of middle adulthood as we cast and recast our central characters in more specific and expansive roles, striving for greater harmony, balance and reconciliation between them. Also increasingly emerging during this time is a concern with our myth's denouement or ending and, in particular, a striving to construct our story in a way that ensures we leave a legacy that will, in some sense, survive us. We seek, in McAdams' (1997: 224) words, 'to fashion personal myths that defy the most basic convention of stories – that an ending is really the end. We seek endings that furnish new beginnings through which the self may live on. In our endings, we seek to defy the end, like the genes that replicate themselves from one generation to the next. As hopelessly narcissistic as it may seem, we are all looking, in one way or another, for immortality'.

- *Narrative evaluation.* Narrative construction does not cease at the end of middle adulthood. As we strive to make sense of changing life circumstances and new concerns, revision and reconstruction of our life story continues. Nonetheless, for older people there may come a time when story review replaces story making as the central concern. We begin to look back and evaluate the life story we have created. Erikson's notion of ego integrity involves the eventual acceptance, valuing and cherishing of our own life story, despite its shortcomings and limitations. To reject our story as unworthy is to experience despair.

In sum, McAdams offers a theory of how we create identities through narrative. In childhood we develop the raw materials or building blocks that we will later use to construct our narrative; during adolescence we make a first attempt to formulate a coherent narrative of our self; and we spend the adult years developing and refining the characters in our story, striving to bring opposing parts of our story together, to link our story to wider society, and to anticipate our story's end. For McAdams, personal identity in the modern world is a life story: 'If you want to know me, then you must know my story, for my story defines who I am. If *I* want to know *myself*, to gain insight into the meaning of my own life, then I, too, must come to know my own story' (McAdams, 1997: 11). Counselling can be seen as a setting for the discovering, creating and telling of clients' stories.

Story form

McAdams' idea of 'basic narrative tone' suggests that the type of life story we tell will be either basically optimistic or basically pessimistic.

However, this is not a hard-and-fast rule, nor is it the only influence on what type of story we tell. Salmon suggests that we expect (often implicitly) people at different life stages to see life according to different story forms – and that this is socially reinforced. We have, in other words, norms and expectations about how our understanding of life as a story typically evolves across the life course.

For the most part we want and expect children to see life in an optimistic way – we want them to experience the world as a basically trustworthy, secure place where they can enjoy a happy, successful and fulfilling life. Stories we tell children, especially very young children, tend to have a clear and optimistic ending – 'happy ever after'. Sometimes these stories are over-sanitised and at odds with the difficult realities of many children's lives, and in response to this, much more children's literature now engages with the real-life issues and transitions that they may face – loss through bereavement or parental divorce, prejudice, disability, bullying, abuse. In much of this literature the characters eventually reach a satisfactory, albeit perhaps not perfect, resolution. The message is still basically optimistic, or at least hopeful: life may have difficulties, but they are manageable.

With regard to adolescents, society considers it desirable and appropriate, suggests Salmon, for them to adopt an optimistic, romantic view of life – a viewpoint whereby the future is seen as a series of challenges and threats that can be overcome by the forces of idealism, love and personal commitments. We are concerned when children and adolescents adopt a pessimistic stance and lack hope for the future, seeing it as an 'off time' worldview, perhaps the consequence of 'off time' experiences – for example having received inadequate nurturing or having been overburdened with responsibilities we see as more appropriate to the adult years.

Whilst we like to see adolescents as full of hope for the future, we generally expect them through early adulthood to develop a more 'realistic' perspective on the life course. The 40-year-old who still sees life as a romantic adventure may be criticised as 'naïve' or 'unworldly', and as needing, perhaps, to 'get real'. More realistic 'adult' understandings of life involve acceptance of the inevitability of some measure of disappointment and failure – although a degree of optimism may not be frowned on. The tragic story form explains defeat in terms of personal shortcomings; the ironic story form in terms of the hopelessness of our situation.

The relationship between life stage and world-view as reflected in different story forms is not, however, absolute, and as individuals we do not necessarily adhere exclusively to one story form in presenting our personal narrative to the world. When we use narratives to present ourselves to others, the form a story takes may vary according to the situation and goals of the storyteller. Thus, narratives told as a romance, with narrators overcoming obstacles to achieve a goal, may represent (Gergen, 1988) attempts by the narrators to present themselves as heroes living in a world of treachery or danger. Listeners would be expected to be enthralled and admiring of such a protagonist. Similarly, the tragedy may be designed to elicit sympathy, and the comedy a companionable spirit of solidarity and harmony (Gergen, 1988). In these ways, narratives, although statements about ourselves, fulfil important social functions.

Story styles

Rather than focusing on the building blocks of the overall life narrative (as does McAdams) or the overarching story form (as does Salmon), Janine Roberts (1994), a family therapist, looks at how particular stories within that narrative are told – how complete are they, how fluid are they, and how do they relate to other stories the client tells? In total she distinguishes six story styles: *intertwined*, *isolated*, *incomplete*, *unspoken*, *frozen* and *evolving*. With intertwined and isolated stories the most salient issue concerns the amount and nature of resonance between different stories; with incomplete and silenced stories the issue is about gaps – why and how they occurred, whether they can be filled, and the implications of so doing; and with frozen and evolving stories the issue is about movement and change versus stagnation and fixity.

- *Intertwined stories.* Intertwined stories resonate – either because of their similarities or because of their differences – with stories of another time and/or place. This can be a wonderful resource. Through such resonance we can use the stories we have already lived and heard to understand our present and decide how to act: 'I would never treat anyone the way I was treated as a child', we might say – or, 'I want you to enjoy the same support as I had in a similar situation'.

  However, stories may become enmeshed, or possibly soldered together, rather than merely intertwined:

With intertwined stories people often experience time as collapsed – what is happening in the present is lived in some ways as if it were happening in the past. As one story resonates with another, meaning is passed between them, even though it may not fit the situation. When stories are too richly cross-joined, the first story seems to overwhelm the second story with interpretations of behavior and actions and with its own emotional field. People involved in the second story then find few possibilities of coming to their own meaning-making of the events in their lives. The meaning has already been passed from the first story. (Roberts, 1994: 14)

The task for counsellor and client may then be to unravel 'this tangled web we weave', so that each story can stand on its own, with its uniqueness and integrity respected. Roberts (1994) suggests questions to help therapists and clients work with intertwined stories – as shown in Box 5.1.

Box 5.1: Exploring intertwined stories

With intertwined stories the goal is to help people discover and name the links between events in their life and the meaning they ascribe to them. It is then easier to work out the significance of the meaning that is spilling over between the stories, whether it is appropriate and helpful. Relevant questions (Roberts, 1994) include the following.

- When you think of or tell this story about your life, what other stories are triggered in your mind?
- What is it about the story that makes you think of the other story(ies)? Is it the emotional content of the story, the place where it is set, certain words that are used, the people involved, the way the story is told?
- How do these stories influence or affect each other? Is this influence helpful or not?
- How would telling the story be different if it didn't trigger the other stories?

- *Isolated stories.* Just as stories can become overly intertwined, so too may they be overly isolated. If we are blind to the ways in which our stories are linked then we cannot learn from our experience. Instead, we are forever reinventing the wheel, as it were. Exploring the ways in which stories from different life stages or from different areas of our life might be linked (see Box 5.2) lends greater coherence to the meanings and interpretations we give to our experience. It is the antithesis of the extreme compartmentalisation of our lives into categories such as work/play, home/school or now/then.

Box 5.2: Exploring isolated stories

The counsellor's role with stories told in isolation is to help clients explore whether there might be unrecognised reverberations with other stories. People may then be able to plot meaning-making across different contexts and times. Relevant questions (Roberts, 1994) include these.

- If you were to connect this story to other stories in your life, what stories might it be linked to?
- How would the first story be different if you made this connection? Would it be different in emotional tone, in outcome, in the characters that people it, in the possibilities it suggests for the future?
- What might the effect be on your life if the first story continues to stand alone?

- *Incomplete stories.* Through a range of disruptions – changing school or job, geographic moves, family break-ups – we may lose contact with our stability zones: the 'locations, symbols, people, and activities' (Roberts, 1994: 16) that might otherwise inhabit our stories. In the upheaval of moving house, photos, letters and other memorabilia may be thrown out or lost. Family rituals and reunions, whilst they may constrain and confine us, also help us know who we are. When parents divorce, children may lose contact with one set of grandparents, thereby losing access to a range of stories about the family. Stories are patchy (McLeod, 1997) or incomplete, with crucial episodes missing, stages skipped and causal links omitted. Clients with minimal information about their past may need help in excavating and building what stories they can about their history, and/or in imagining what the irretrievable stories might have been, and what this would have meant – see Box 5.3.

Box 5.3: Exploring incomplete stories

Where there are gaps in clients' information about a part of their life, a counsellor's role might be to help fill those gaps by assisting clients find, assimilate and interpret the stories that surround their life. They might, for example, ask (Roberts, 1994) the following questions.

- Who can you go to for information about your life around the time period of the story?
- What pictures, symbols, clothing or other artefacts do you have from that period of your life that might stimulate remembrance?

A more important role for counsellors may, however, be to encourage clients in exploration of the possible implications of attempting to fill in the gaps in their stories.

- How do you imagine your life might be different if the story were more complete and detailed?
- If the story had not been interrupted, how do you think it might have developed?

There may be missing parts in a story that can never be filled by 'facts'. Counsellors may help clients furnish such voids with imagined possibilities – with hitherto unacknowledged fears and dreams.

- If you were to fill out this story, how would you like it to be?
- What difference would it make in your life if you filled it out in this way?
- Who would you like to tell your story to; when, and under what circumstances? How might this telling affect your life?

- *Unspoken stories.* Unspoken stories are perhaps the most difficult and potentially risky stories to work with. Whereas the gaps in incomplete stories can be openly acknowledged and addressed, stories that have been silenced or are secret present complex issues of safety and disclosure: 'When there are secret stories in a family, people live with a subterranean text. Meaning is unclear, and there are often hidden alliances and coalition' (Roberts, 1994: 18). Counsellors must listen and pay attention to the unspoken: 'it is the continuous backdrop for that which can be told' (p. 9). Counselling can offer an arena where narratives can be put together (see Box 5.4) in a safe and protected way, and where clients can address the questions of whether, when, where and how secret stories might be shared with others.

Box 5.4: Exploring unspoken stories

With stories that have been kept secret or have been silenced there may be painstaking work to be done in discovering and acknowledging the stories, and also in deciding what to do with them – who should hear the stories, when, and with what support for both the teller and listeners. Relevant questions (Roberts, 1994) include those below.

- In what ways has this story been silenced? By whom and why?
- What effect has this silencing had on you? On others in your family?
- What do you think the effects would be of continuing *not* to tell the story?
- What would happen if this story were to be told? What would need to happen to ensure safe disclosure?

- *Frozen stories.* Frozen stories are told repeatedly in the same way. They are static, rigid and unbending. Their content and assumed meaning is so familiar and unquestioned that we may be blinkered to alternative stances – it is as if there is only one way of telling the story, and, indeed, only one story to tell. 'But that's the way it is', we might say to ourselves. 'It always has been, and always will be'. A role for counsellors (see Box 5.5) is to help clients liberate themselves from the constraints of such frozen or rigidly told stories – melting the ice, one might say.

Box 5.5: Exploring frozen stories

When clients' stories are frozen or rigid, counsellors can help them to tell their stories from different vantage points, supporting the incorporation of alternative perspectives into the tales. They may also explore novel aspects or different endings to a frozen story, and encourage the widening of the repertoire of stories that are told. Questions to ask might be (Roberts, 1994) as follows.

- How long has this story been told in this way? Why do you think it took this form?
- For whom would it be hardest to change this story? Easiest?
- If this story were to change, what would be the implications for you? For other people?
- How might you want to change the story? What would help you do this?

- *Evolving stories.* From a life course perspective, a role for counsellors can be seen as the nurturance and encouragement of evolving stories (Box 5.6). Not only do personal, family and other cultural stories need to be told, but they need to be told (and heard) across time, enabling them to be understood on different levels. As we develop, we are able to make meanings in different ways cognitively, and also draw on new knowledge and sets of life experiences to help us to interpret events (McAdams, 1997). In this way we can both sense our movement through life, and be anchored in our history. Stories from our family and community locate us in our lives:

> They tell us where we have come from and articulate central themes and values. At the same time, they can provide the foundation for new stories, new ideas and beliefs to be shared. If we do not know the old stories, it is sometimes hard to move on to the new ones, because we are unsure of what it is we want to keep from our heritage and what it is we want to change. Understanding what has been given to us through the stories in our lives, while having an ongoing dialogue about the new stories that are being created, lets us both hold the past and move on with the present and future (Roberts, 1994: 21).

Box 5.6: Exploring evolving stories

Counsellors can help clients identify those of their stories that have been and continue to be evolving, both as a self-validating experience in itself, and as a vehicle for assisting them reconsider those stories told in other story styles.

- How have your stories changed over time?
- What in your family and/or community life supported this evolving process?
- If you were to tell central family stories five years from now, how do you think they would be told? Ten years from now?

Adopting a narrative stance need not be incompatible with a stage-based perspective on the life course. Earlier, the age-associated stages involved in the construction and development of personal narratives (McAdams, 1997) were summarised. Similarly, Cohler (1982) presents a person's life narrative as continually being reorganised on the basis of subsequent experiences, arguing that if narrative coherence cannot be maintained, the individual will experience 'feelings of fragmentation or personal disintegration' (Cohler, 1982: 215). He goes on to propose that three life-stage-associated transformations are especially likely to provoke narrative disruption. These are the transitions from:

- *early to middle childhood* – with its associated cognitive and social developments;
- *childhood to adolescence and young adulthood* – denoting the increased capacity for abstract thought, and the ability to conceive past, present and future as a connected narrative; and
- *early to middle adulthood* – associated with a heightened awareness of the finitude of life.

The first transition is linked to the shift in cognitive and social processes that occurs between the ages of five and seven years. The child becomes increasingly able to make use of concrete logical thought, to understand situations from another person's perspective and to understand three-way relationships. This results in the development of a markedly different world-view, and triggers a profound transformation of the child's understanding of his or her place within it. The 'old' stories, as it were, are no longer adequate explanations, and must be reformulated. Adolescence – with its physiological changes, the cognitive development of formal operations and changed relationships within an increasingly complex social environment – is identified as a second point of major transformation in the personal narrative. It is encapsulated in Erikson's notion of the psychosocial identity crisis.

Both the early to middle childhood transformation, and the transformation of the adolescent identity crisis are associated with maturation – both biological and psychological maturation and the socially shared understanding of the significance of such developments. In Cohler's third transformational period, which accompanies the transition from early to middle adulthood, maturation plays a far less significant part. Instead, its nature is largely socially determined and involves assessment and reassessment of the self in relation to the timing and passage of normatively defined social milestones. Its timing is also linked to the developing awareness of the reality of a finite lifetime. Not only is it the chronological 'mid-point' of the expected life cycle, but both the expected and anticipated death of the older generation (in particular, parents) and the 'untimely' death of contemporaries, serve as constant reminders of mortality. Cohler postulates, although does not develop to the same degree, the existence of a further transformation accompanying the transition from middle to old age. This is consistent with evidence of the particular importance of reminiscence in old age – 'getting the story straight', and striving to rework events into a coherent, fulfilling life narrative. The overall pattern is also consistent with Levinson's concept of an evolving life structure, with transformational periods marking key structure-changing phases. Think back to whether your responses to Activity 3: Life chapters provide any support for the existence of these transformational transitions.

Although the narratives within our society can give guidance and directionality to our lives, they may be imperfect guides (Cochran, 1997) – as, for example, if we were to accept uncritically the 'disengagement' narrative that it is normal and desirable to withdraw from significant roles as we age. Like an individual's life structure (Levinson et al., 1978; Levinson, 1986), cultural narratives may become out of date and no longer compatible with the prevailing conditions of life. 'Lifted from conditions of life to which they did apply, these narratives might be described as anachronistic, impoverished, or distorted' (Cochran, 1997: 137). The notion of career choice as a once-and-for-all decision and of career development as a smooth, upward progression would constitute one such outmoded narrative.

Furthermore, narratives may conflict such that, to use Cochran's phrase, we may 'be torn between two narratives' (p. 137). A Western narrative emphasising self-fulfilment may conflict with an Eastern one that emphasises family obligation, such that second-generation immigrants may feel they have to choose between isolation from their family and stultification of personal dreams.

Within any one community the cultural narratives of some subcultures may be more readily enacted than others. Gay and lesbian youth may, for example, find their narrative less easy to enact in the heterosexual ambience of many school and college communities. Furthermore, there may be situations for which no adequate cultural narratives exist. Thus, there may be no cultural narratives to guide women or ethnic minorities trying to move into careers that have traditionally been dominated by white, middle-class males. With time, the individual role models provided by pioneers who break through barriers through personally derived solutions may develop into new cultural narratives.

Some authors (for example, Berne, 1975; Gustafson, 1992) propose that we each develop a core narrative, or personal myth, that is the central or singular (Spence, 1987) story behind the various stories we tell, and which we repeat in different relationships at different points across the life course. However, the narrative perspective in general assumes we are able to generate multiple storylines to accommodate and account for our experiences (McLeod, 1997). Any one account is likely to be only a provisional interpretation. Thus, Viney and Bousfield (1991) describe the core narrative as more like a suggestive hypothesis than a confirmed generalisation, likening it to a 'statement of best fit'. It is not the only statement that could be made, but it is one that is plausible. A core narrative may be resilient, but not inviolable.

Although the concept of narrative provides an integrative framework in its own right, it is perfectly possible to talk about a life course perspective without invoking the metaphor of story. The final chapter reviews what a life course perspective entails; and it can be seen that a narrative fulfils each of the key criteria.

6

Taking a life course perspective

'*Composing a life involves a continual reimagining of the future and reinterpretation of the past to give meaning to the present.*'

(Mary Catherine Bateson, 1990)

To take a life course perspective involves implicitly or explicitly signing up to four key principles as summarised by Shanahan et al. (2003). These are the principles of *lifelong processes*; of *lives in place and time*; of *human agency*; and of *timing of experiences*.

- A life course perspective normalises change, with the *principle of lifelong processes* not only recognising change and development as possibilities throughout the life span, but also holding that the quality of any one life stage is influenced both by trajectories extending back into the past and also by anticipations of the future. To paraphrase the epigraph that heads this chapter (Bateson, 1990) – the present is given meaning in the context of a past that is continually being reinterpreted and a future that is continually being reimagined. Counselling provides a site for these processes of exploration and renegotiation of our past, present and future; and the life course provides a framework for their location and conceptualisation.

  A life course perspective is a broad church, encouraging what can be termed 'both/and' rather than 'either/or' thinking. Thus, across the whole life course life changes are seen as almost inevitably involving both gains and losses. The balance, or ratio, between gains and losses will, however, vary across different life events or transitions and across different life stages. Whilst the suggestion (Baltes, 1987; Heckhausen and Lang, 1996) that for many older people the balance shifts towards losses rather than gains seemingly gives some credence to the stereotype of old age as a period of decline, this stance still allows for the possibility, indeed probability, of gains as well. Thus, life course trajectories can be both mutable and multidirectional.

- The concept of the life course is an inherently and distinctively social concept, as evidenced in the *principle of lives in place and time*. People's lives are embedded in and shaped by the environments and historical times in which they occur. It follows from this that clients are best seen and understood in a changing and evolving context – as part of, and inseparable from, a particular family, social network and culture.

Since environments vary across time and place, accounts of a 'typical' life course can never hold timeless or universal sway. Whilst retaining some similarities, the tasks associated with different life stages will vary across different cultural groups. Nor do these tasks necessarily remain the same. Havighurst amended his lists of life-stage-related developmental tasks several times during his long career (Havighurst, 1972; Chickering and Havighurst, 1981). The need to do so again will continue. It is a never-ending story. Those who fear that concepts of normative life stages or developmental tasks represent too prescriptive and controlling a view of the life course might find solace in this, although it is also important to be alert to unwarranted slippage from descriptive accounts of 'what is' to directive dictates about 'what ought' to be.

By emphasising the individual's embeddedness within and inter-action with a multifaceted physical and interpersonal environment, a life course perspective also emphasises the promotion of intervention as a multidisciplinary, and multiprofessional enterprise, discouraging disciplinary and professional insularity. It echoes Proctor and Inskipp's (1999) plea for 'post-tribalism' to be counselling's millennium gift to clients. Whilst tribalism, in the form of adherence to a core theoretical model, can bestow a sense of security and identity on counsellors, clients and their contexts are gloriously diverse. The life course provides a framework and language for accommodating this diversity.

A life course perspective also indicates, hand-in-hand with a sympathy for post-tribalism, the need for multiprofessional teams – as described by Twining (1996) in relation to work with older people. When people are coping with more than one problem at once then they are likely to need more than one sort of help at the same time. In these situations the model of exclusive treatment is much less likely to be appropriate. Having said that, there is no assumption that the creation of multidisciplinary teams is either easy or straightforward. Different treatment goals and different conceptualisations of the client–practitioner relationship ensures that there is much to be discussed and negotiated. It may be that the concept of the life course can provide a framework for such debates, in the same way that the Ethical Framework of the British Association for Counselling and Psychotherapy (BACP) (2002) directs attention to the level of principle rather than detailing a potentially endless list of 'dos' and 'don'ts'.

■ Although people's circumstances – personal, social and historical – place them within a particular opportunity structure (Roberts, 1977), each of us is also instrumental in constructing our own life course through the choices we make. Also, the relation between person and environment is reciprocal. Not only does the environment impact on the person, but the person is influential in creating and modifying the circumstances and manner in which they live. Through their choices, through purposeful actions, and through the allocation of meanings, people construct their own life course. This is the *principle of human agency*. It is the area in which the individual has room to manoeuvre and in which client and counsellor can address the task of providing – in the words of the BACP's (2002: 1) definition of counselling – 'an opportunity for the client to work towards living in a way he or she experiences as more satisfying and resourceful'.

Another facet of the 'both/and' perspective is that individuals are seen as bringing both helpful and hindering factors to situations. Interventions – including counselling – can be seen as aimed at modifying the balance between these factors, such that the strength of the facilitating factors is increased and the strength of the hindering factors is minimised. The strategy of force field analysis (see Box 6.1) is grounded in this principle.

Box 6.1: Force field analysis

The technique of force field analysis can be used to help plan and evaluate change. It is based on the premise that a problem situation can be thought of as a state of equilibrium between the forces for change and the forces resisting change. The identification of these forces, their direction (that is, helping or hindering the desired change), their strength and how they can be modified is the *force field analysis*. The diagram below illustrates the basic idea. Facilitating forces (both personal assets and external resources) push the person towards the desired outcome, whilst the forces resisting the change (both personal shortcomings and external obstacles) push the person towards a less desired outcome.

Facilitating forces		**Restraining forces**	
−			+
Worst	⟶	CURRENT ◀	Ideal
possible	⟶	STATE ◀	state
state	⟶	◀	

Conducting a force field analysis involves the following stages.

(1) Summarise the desired outcome of the change – the ideal state – in clear, concrete terms.

(2) Identify:

    (i) forces hindering or blocking movement towards the ideal state;

    (ii) forces facilitating movement towards the ideal state.

(3) Develop:

    (i) ways of removing or reducing the strength of the restraining forces;

    (ii) ways of increasing the strength of the facilitating forces.

(4) Identify any costs or negative consequences of different courses of action.

(5) Select a specific course of action.

(6) Establish criteria for measuring progress.

■ The fourth core principle of the life course perspective – the *principle of timing of experiences* – links the discussion back to the principle of lifelong processes in that it is concerned with the location of experiences within the life span. It holds that the impact and meaning of the events and transitions that comprise a person's life course is contingent upon when in that life they occur. Transitions only really make sense if they are considered in a life course context, for only then is it possible to see the way a person's life moves on and unfolds (Bridges, 1980). Understanding of a particular event or transition needs to be filtered through an awareness of the distinct opportunities and vulnerabilities associated with a client's age, life stage and circumstances.

As an integrating framework, the concept of the life course encourages cross-fertilisation of ideas, pointing to similarities as well as differences between different life stages. Thus, for example, whilst life review is generally seen as a process relevant to late adulthood (Butler, 1963; Lewis and Butler, 1974) with life review therapy an intervention for use with older people (Garland, 1994), it is a part of all Levinson's structure-changing phases. It has been used as a therapeutic frame for intervention with clients who are HIV positive (Borden, 1989; Vaughan and Kinnier, 1996), and is a significant element in life story work (Ryan and Walker, 1997) with children moving into foster or adoptive homes. Despite the multifarious changes that accompany our passage through the life course, there are notable similarities across all life stages. Thus, Bee (1994) concluded that life satisfaction can be predicted by more or less the same four factors irrespective of life stage, namely: adequate interpersonal support; a sense of control; a low incidence of 'off time' or unplanned events; and adequate financial means.

Importance of client's age

Although the wholesale transfer of perspectives and strategies from one age group to another may be inappropriate, the 'universals' that are common across all counselling situations may be as important as the 'particulars', and are what individual counsellors bring to any extension of their work into new arenas – including clients of different ages or life stages. There are a number of significant, and often related, issues that have different implications for clients of different ages.

■ *Power.* Our age gives us varying degrees of access to social and support resources, including counselling. Children and the very old often have limited direct power over the services they receive. Counsellors, through being overwhelmingly in the years of young and middle adulthood, possess important reins of power within a society where social power is strongly influenced by earnings and financial wherewithal.

- *Client's developmental status.* Clients of different ages and life stages will have different psychological, cognitive and sensory capacities, and these will influence both what issues they bring to counselling and what approaches are most appropriate. Counsellors working with children and young adolescents need to be sensitive to their level of verbal and cognitive development as well as their level of emotional maturity. With clients in late adulthood, decreasing sensory capacity (notably sight and hearing) may need to be taken into account along with the declining cognitive functioning that may – but does not inevitably – accompany the ageing process.

- *Cohort factors.* Each generation within a society is in some ways unique, having grown up in a particular economic, political and social environment, and having particular shared experiences. The age difference between client and counsellor is one of the factors influencing the extent to which they share direct experience of key events on the world and domestic stage, and have been exposed to similar social norms. Clients of different ages to the counsellor – be they significantly older or significantly younger – may believe that 'the world is different now' and that the counsellor, being of a different generation, cannot possibly understand what they are experiencing.

- *Client's reaction to the counsellor's age and life stage.* This point is related to transference. Counsellors may (some would argue 'will') unwittingly trigger both conscious and unconscious reminders in clients of other relationships in which they have been involved. Parental transference – whereby clients re-experience and re-enact with the counsellor aspects of the relationship they had with their parents – is consistent with the power relationship between counsellor and client and with the life stage relationship when the counsellor is significantly older than the client. For older clients, the transference may reflect their relationship with their children or grandchildren. Whilst children may see a counsellor as an authority figure, an older person may consider the same person to be inexperienced and/or presumptive in assuming they have anything to offer: 'the client may have at least twice as much relevant experience of the ageing process as the counsellor. It is hardly appropriate to cast the novice [that is, the counsellor] as the expert. Rather it is about trying to help clients assimilate the realities of ageing' (Twining, 1996: 379).

- *Counsellor's reaction to the client's age and life stage.* This point relates to the issue of countertransference. Counsellors need to develop awareness of what issues are triggered in themselves by the age and life stage of the client. Clients may present scenarios or exhibit behaviours that in many ways mirror issues also being addressed by the counsellor in his or her own life. Counsellors may identify with the issues faced by clients at a similar life stage to themselves. Younger clients may bring counsellors' own children to mind, and older clients may remind them of their parents or grandparents, possibly providing glimpses of problems and challenges that may lie ahead not only for their parents and grandparents, but also for themselves. Supervision is crucial in providing counsellors with an arena in which to explore these responses and with the opportunity to disentangle the personal from the professional.
- *Empathy.* Counsellors may be less able to empathise readily with clients of different ages to themselves. By the same token, they may need to be wary of over-identifying with clients seen as 'similar to me'. Furthermore, it cannot be assumed that clients see counsellors of the same age as 'like them'. A counsellor of a similar age to themselves can emphasise a client's sense of personal inadequacy – 'how come he/she is coping so well, whereas I need help'. The myth of the superhuman counsellor can come into play here. Finally, it is important that the significance of age is not overemphasised. Age is, of course, only one amongst many key variables along which clients (and counsellors) vary; albeit a variable that has received less explicit attention than the variables of sex, ethnicity and class.

Biographical interviewing

And now we come to the final Activity Trail exercise – Activity 12: Biographical interviewing. It is grounded in the data-collection method of Daniel Levinson and his colleagues, whose work has been referred to a good many times during the course of this text. Their technique of Intensive Biographical Interviewing provides a bridge between academic research and counselling practice. Levinson's (1996: 8–9) comments on the process are both concise and wide-ranging:

> The primary aim of Intensive Biographical Interviewing is to enable the participant to tell her life story from childhood to the present. The word

'story' is of fundamental importance here. It is common in academic settings to say that we are getting a 'history' – a clinical case history, developmental history, work history, or family history. Such histories focus selectively on particular events and issues of importance to the history taker. When we want to learn about the life course, however, the term 'story' is more appropriate. The person telling her story is identified by the researcher, and experiences herself not as a patient, client, or research subject (that is, object), but as *participant* in a joint effort. The participant is more freely and fully engaged when she feels invited to tell her story in her own terms, and when she feels that the interviewer is a truly interested listener/participant in the storytelling. The story is the medium in which various messages are delivered – about joys and sorrows, times of abundance and times of depletion, the sense of wasting one's life or of using it well, efforts at building, maintaining, and ending significant relationships.

The task of telling the story is mainly the participant's. The interviewer's task is to facilitate the storytelling: to listen actively and empathically, to affirm the value of what she or he is hearing, to offer questions and comments that help the participant give a fuller, more coherent, and more textured account. The biographical interviewer is different from the survey interviewer, whose task is to obtain specific information on specific topics, and from the psychotherapist, whose task is to help the participant understand and modify her inner problems. The interviewer's interest in the life story and responsiveness to it are critical factors in the participant's readiness to tell it, especially those parts that are deeply satisfying and/or painful.

Activity 12: Biographical interviewing

In contrast to Activity 11: Exploring your story, this is an outwardly referenced exercise in that, rather than reflecting on your own life course, you are invited to explore that of another. The 'right' to do this has been earned by your having worked through Activity Trail exercises 1–11. The vehicle through which it can be achieved is that of biographical interviewing.

Biographical interviewing is an approach to interviewing that aims to combine aspects of the research and the clinical interview. Although certain topics are to be covered, the interviewer is sensitive to the feelings expressed by interviewees, and attempts to explore themes in ways that have meaning for each participant – following rather than leading. Whilst both interviewers and participants have a defined role, with the constraints that this implies, the relationship between them is one of equality, both being able to comment on the process, and interviewers as well as participants being able to respond on the basis of their own personal experiences.

It is suggested that you find a person to interview; and spend in the region of an hour talking through (and ideally tape-recording) aspects of their life experience. In preparation you might ask them to complete a Life chapters exercise or a Lifeline (as in Activities 3 and 5, respectively) and use this as a starting point for your exploration. Afterwards, this interview can be used as a basis for evaluating a number of the ideas and concepts introduced in earlier chapters. In effect, it is an exercise in testing their meaningfulness for you.

As to whom you choose to interview – well, the choice is vast. Interviewing a family member can be fascinating. For a parent, grandparent or other relative of an 'older' generation to share with you how they saw their life when they were at the age you are now can be moving, insightful and humbling. Often the exercise triggers a deepening of understanding, empathy and closeness. A sibling or childhood friend can also prove an excellent choice of interviewee, especially when it provides the opportunity to learn about another's slant on events and experiences that you have shared. Alternatively, interviewing an acquaintance or a recent friend or colleague will often both deepen the relationship and make apparent how small a part of the person you knew beforehand.

As with counselling, the contract between yourself and your interviewee is important, with the issues of informed consent and confidentiality being crucial. Before undertaking the interview you will need to ensure that the interviewee realises what is involved – how long the interview is likely to be, why you are doing it, what it's about and the sort of topic that will be addressed. You may wish to negotiate with regard to the possibility of tape-recording the interview. In this case, the issue of ownership of the tape, who will have access to it (this will be important if the interview is part of a course assignment), and what will happen to it afterwards. It is also crucial to ensure that interviewees understand that the interview is not a counselling session and that they have the right to refuse to answer any question and to stop the interview if they so wish.

Although it may appear daunting, to conduct a biographical interview is rarely an unrewarding exercise.

So, although Levinson distinguishes Intensive Biographical Interviewing from psychotherapy, he recognises that it shares characteristics with therapeutic encounters. He also links Biographical Interviewing to the exploration of life story. McAdams' interview schedule, which formed the basis of Activity 11: Exploring your story, can, by the same token, be seen as a method for developing a picture of a person's life structure. Activity 11 asked you to reflect on your own life story, but the questions can also be asked of someone else in a biographical interview.

Finale

And so the links go on. The book closes in much the same way as it began – with a vignette that illustrates life course issues coming together in the peculiarities of a particular life. Having read it through, see to what extent you can apply life course concepts as a framework for exploring Ben's situation. Concepts to think about include:

- the notion of an evolving life structure;
- life stage;
- developmental tasks – and their origin;
- life events – on time and off time, normative and non-normative;
- transitions and turning points – sudden and gradual, chosen and imposed, positive and negative;
- stability zones – and their disruption;
- support convoys;
- the settings that form a part of the life course.

Ben had enjoyed a challenging gap year between school and university. He had worked hard to earn money to pay for his volunteer placement teaching in Vietnam – and his parents had been willing and able to make up the shortfall. Excited, but at times over-whelmed, by the cultural shock of life in Asia, he had relished the new experiences. However, it was the weekly get-togethers with other volunteers and, in particular, the e-mails from home that kept him going through the (almost) inevitable periods of loneliness and stomach upsets. At difficult moments he was thankful to know that if things really got too difficult, he could always go home earlier than planned. This, however, had not proved necessary – the agency had sorted out for him some initial problems with his placement, and now, some 20 months later, he was happily settled in his second year at university. During the summer vacation he had a week's holiday in France with his parents and younger brother, and a month of touring with the local youth orchestra of which he had been a member for three or four years whilst at school. Both trips had been great, but he realised that now his main reference group was his university friends. Time spent with his parents, and even with friends from his home town, largely represented a welcome break from what he now saw as his 'real' life. His relationship with his brother remained in limbo – Michael, some five years younger than Ben, currently seemed still a part of their parents' world; but Ben anticipated a time when he and Michael would both take their places in a generation that reached adulthood in the twenty-first rather than the twentieth century. Three months later – and to his total surprise – Ben's parents separated and the family home was put on the market. Two months after that, his brother was involved in a serious car accident from which he is unlikely to make a full recovery. It was at this point that Ben approached the university counselling service.

This vignette sees Ben as part of several interlocking settings – home, volunteer agency and host country, university, orchestra. Each comprises a complex system of spoken and unspoken demands, norms and expectations that both complement and contradict each other. The relationship is two-way – with the individual influencing the environment as well as the environment influencing the individual. In terms of life stage, Ben is a fledgling adult. He has – outwardly at least – successfully negotiated several aspects of separation from the parental home, and the establishment of an independent lifestyle and identity. However, in the process, there has been significant disruption and diminution of his support networks. It remains to be seen whether his new friendship bonds are sufficiently strong and stable to constitute an effective support convoy.

Ben has faced a number of the normative transitions and life events typically associated with his life stage. Whilst these may have been challenging and problematic, there was also the sense that they were appropriate issues to be facing at that stage of his life – they were 'on time' events. His brother's accident, by contrast, was a non-normative event. It could have occurred at any time. The life stage of leaving school and entering university is part of a transitional phase which Levinson described as the Early Adult Transition, leading to a more stable phase – Entering the Adult World. Michael's accident is likely to disrupt Ben's smooth passage through these normative life stages. It may well mark a turning point in his own life as well as his brother's. The disability that Michael's accident seems likely to lead to challenges Ben's taken-for-granted assumptions about the nature of his relationship with his brother, and how it would develop in the future. To lose health and vigour as an adolescent is an off time event that few have anticipated or developed resources for managing.

The aim of this book has been to foster awareness of and sensitivity to life course issues. If it has succeeded then you will have added new concepts and models to your repertoire of professional skills that, hopefully, will have been reflected in differences between your analysis of this vignette and your initial response to Maria's story in Chapter 1. Hopefully the book has increased your appreciation of each person's life course (including your own and those of your clients) as both universally human and completely unique. In adopting the principle of lifelong processes, a life course perspective considers the specific events, processes and interpretative meanings in an individual's developmental path. In adopting the principle of lives in place and time, it takes both an ecological and historical perspective – considering the transactions between an individual and the personal, social and cultural networks in which he or she is embedded, and ways in which a person's life is shaped by and responsive to historical events and milieux. The principle of human agency acknowledges the role of individuals in the creation of their own life story, thereby speaking to the uniqueness of a particular life. Acknowledging the importance of the timing of experiences, the fourth principle of the life course perspective, reiterates the point that, although they are by no means the whole story, age and life stage do matter.

Counselling places the specialness and uniqueness of each client centre stage. A life course perspective both recognises this and offers a framework that can help to rescue us from the loneliness of such singularity. A frequent fear in counselling and therapy is fear of the unknown. However, the events, transitions and stages within a life share many similarities both with other events, transitions and stages the person has faced, and with those faced by others. Highlighting this, and looking at the ways in which previous transitions have been dealt with successfully, may provide comfort, build confidence in meeting new challenges, provide a basis for future actions, and promote a sense of contact with people of other places and times.

Appendix: Commentaries on the Activity Trail exercises

First, a disclaimer: this appendix does not comprise a series of 'model answers' to a series of 'test questions' represented by the Activity Trail. Indeed, a number of the commentaries include several more questions. Rather, these commentaries are designed to aid your reflection on the activities – examining and trying to make sense of the responses that you gave. They represent the third stage in David Kolb's (1984) cycle of experiential learning, a model that conceptualises learning as a continuous process grounded in experience:

- immediate *concrete experience* is seen as the basis for
- *reflection and observation;*
- from these observations *abstract concepts* are developed and then
- *actively tested*, giving rise to
- a new *concrete experience.*

Since this last experience is different from that which initiated the learning cycle, the model is best represented as a spiral rather than a circle (there is a link here to pictorial metaphors, as alluded to in Activity 1). Learning occurs in the gap between experience and concept. Experience provides the material that allows us to modify our concepts – that is, to learn. It is my assumption that the first stage of learning resides where Kolb places it – in the concrete emotional experiences that make up your life course in general, and, in particular, your experience of becoming and being a counsellor. It is this experience that the activities draw upon. The activities themselves represent the 'Reflective observation' stage of the learning cycle, although – as with both life stages and transitions – the boundaries between the stages blend into one another. The activities themselves may be, at least in part, concrete experiences, and may well trigger abstract conceptualisations before you turn to the pages of this appendix. But this is what the commentaries are primarily concerned with – the garnering and interpretation of your responses into theoretical constructs. My hope is that you will then be able to take these insights and use them (or 'actively experiment' with them, to use Kolb's terminology) in your counselling practice.

I hope it is clear that the exercises making up the Activity Trail are not written in stone. Nor are they the only exercises that could have been chosen. They are a means to an end rather than an end in themselves. Some of the activities focus on your own personal experience, others ask you to reflect on your understanding of your clients' world. All can be adapted to your own particular needs. If the questions in the Activity Trail exercises do not address your particular concerns, then compose your own questions – they are the trigger rather than the answer, and should be amended to meet your particular needs and interests.

Activity 1: Metaphors of the life course

The framework offered by the notion of the life course provides a conceptual bridge between individuals and the society in which they live their lives. Metaphorical images of the life course reflect an emphasis on one or more of four core principles that characterise a life course perspective (Shanahan et al., 2003); namely:

- change is a cumulative and lifelong human process;
- human lives are embedded in and shaped by both their environment – social, cultural, technological and physical – and the historical time in which they live;
- people construct their own life course – albeit within the constraints and opportunities of personal, social and historical circumstances;
- the impact and meaning of life course experiences hinge on when they occur in a person's life.

In using the metaphor of a river as the opening sentence of our chapter in the *Handbook of Counselling* (Palmer and McMahon, 1997), Ray Woolfe and I strove to capture this dynamic, interactive, multifaceted and mutable quality:

> The life course of each of us can be thought of as a river. On occasions turbulent, but at other times calm, it flows in a particular general direction, whilst deviating here and there from a straight and narrow path. It meets and departs from other rivers or streams along the way, having a momentum of its own whilst both influencing and being influenced by the environment through which it flows. (Sugarman and Woolfe, 1997: 22)

Thus, a river, like the life course, does not reach a static endpoint – it continues to move and change throughout its journey. This movement is not, however, consistent, unidirectional or entirely predetermined; and its path can alter as it wends its way through terrain that can either help or hinder its progress. The river affects the terrain through which it flows; and this terrain, in turn, lends the river a significant amount of its structure. The river changes across seasons and epochs; and the same incident – a drought, a dam, a jetty, for example – will have a different impact depending on the nature of the river at that point in its course. Look back at your own preferred metaphors and think about which of the above principles they best encapsulated.

Whilst different metaphors of the life course may be more or less apt, they are not intended to be unequivocally 'right' or 'wrong'. Whilst all have elements of truth, it is unlikely that any is complete or entirely satisfactory. Instead, they represent different philosophical positions. Salmon (1985: 126) identifies three predominant metaphors, each reflecting a different set of values and assumptions about the nature of the life course: life as a game of cards; life as a natural cycle; and life as a story.

In the 'life as a game of cards' metaphor, winning is the key:

> If there is one metaphor which fits most easily into our society, which is most readily encompassed by our social structures and institutional framework, it is perhaps the metaphor that human life represents a game of cards. Within this image, to be born any particular human being is to be dealt some of the most important cards of the hand that, in living, one must play. To be born into a 'good' family, a family which is middle-class rather than working-class, white rather than black, settled, respectable, prosperous rather than impoverished and insecure – that is to start life with certain key cards. Gender and physique represent other kinds of suit, in which the male card is preferable, but in which card combinations are also important. ... Other cards in the hand are not available at birth, but are acquired later, particularly during childhood and adolescence. They represent factors which will affect later life chances, such as exam passes, kind of schooling, early pregnancy or involvement with the police.

Getting the 'best' cards is not, however, the end of the story: 'A good hand does not inevitably bring success, nor a bad one failure. Winning the game depends on *"playing your cards right"*' (Salmon, 1985: 127). The metaphor of the card game portrays people as fundamentally individualistic and life as basically competitive.

In similar vein, Levinson et al.'s (1978) use of the image of a ladder to convey career development during midlife depicts it as an achievement-oriented, heroic and stereotypically masculine journey – 'onward and upward' we might say. In a paper that challenges stage models of spiritual development as too rational and individualistic, Ray and McFadden (2001) use metaphors of a web and a quilt to convey the more intuitive and relational quality of women's spirituality. Also writing from a feminist perspective, Chaplin (1988: 45) – using the image of a spiral – focuses on development as a process, rejecting the idea of directional movement towards an explicit, coherent 'end-state':

> We grow and change in more of a spiral than in a straight line. We go backwards as well as forwards. Perhaps we can only go forwards if we go

backwards and regress into childlike feelings first. Growth is working with the rhythms, not proceeding from some depressing reality to a perfect harmonious self in the future.

As an image radically different from that of the game-playing metaphor, Salmon (1985: 133) invokes metaphors rooted in the natural world:

> You are, let us imagine, a plant, a shrub, a tree. There you stand, rooted in the soil within which also grow other kinds of plant. That soil nourishes you; but so also do the sunlight and the rain that fall upon you. You have your seasons, each of which is different, all of which are necessary.

The seasons repeat themselves in an everlasting cycle of growth, ripening and decay. Each phase in the cycle has its own meaning and importance. All play their part in making the whole complete. The metaphor of life as a natural cycle has been popular in literature, in everyday life and in academic writings. Thus, Levinson (1996; Levinson et al., 1978) talks of seasons, Super (1980; 1990) of a rainbow and Jung (1972) of middle age as the noon of life. Whilst the organic, developmental aspect to the metaphor is appealing, the metaphor of a natural cycle is also prescriptive. A violet can only become a violet; it cannot choose to become a bluebell or a rabbit. Normality is narrowly defined. The human life course is not, in this metaphor, something we construct for ourselves. Rather, it is our own nature unfolding.

The metaphor of a story, Salmon's third vision of the human life course, has an important place in the present book. It is implicated in several other posts in the Activity Trail (including Activity 3: Life chapters, and Activity 5: Lifeline), and it is elaborated in Chapter 5, Life stories. In contrast to the metaphor of the natural cycle, the metaphor of a story grants us a role as the creator of our own life:

> Each of us lives a story that is ours alone. It is this story which gives our lives their essential shape, defines their heights, their plateaux, their declines, marks out their movement, direction, changes in direction. In living, we tell our stories. ... As authors, we have agency. (Salmon, 1985: 138)

Think back again to the metaphors you were drawn to in Activity 1. It is likely that they reflect your viewpoint on a number of key issues – the relative importance, for example, of 'nature' versus 'nurture'; the interplay between 'continuity' and 'change'; the balance between 'choice' and 'destiny'; or the extent of 'unique' versus 'shared' experiences. What are the strengths and the limitations of the metaphors that you chose? What assumptions do they make about the nature of the life course? What are their implications for practice?

Activity 2: What is an adult?

When used as a class exercise, this activity generally generates much discussion, and, on occasions, a considerable amount of hilarity. Claims along the lines of 'Well, *I'm* certainly not grown up' are often to be heard, sometimes followed by the addendum, 'And I hope I never will be!' – recognition, here, that growing up involves loss as well as gain. Alternatively, the exercise may generate a sense of satisfaction; a feeling that, 'Perhaps I'm more grown up than I thought I was!' Many individuals, and groups, fail to produce what they consider to be a complete or satisfactory definition of adulthood. Asking the supplementary question 'When you were a child, what did you think being an adult meant?' produces some of the more pithy definitions – 'Lipstick and high-heels' being perhaps the most succinct.

Groups of trainee counsellors are by no means the only people who struggle to define what is an adult. Thus, UNESCO in 1976 determined that 'adults are those people whom their own society deems to be adult' (Rogers, 1996: 34) – a somewhat circular definition that nonetheless conveys the social and cultural dimension of the concept. Two educationalists (Knowles, 1990, and Alan Rogers, 1996 – not to be confused with his name-sake Carl) interested in adult learning have also addressed this question.

Knowles (1990) distinguished four different definitions of 'adult', and aspects of each of these are likely to have emerged during your deliberations.

- *Biological adulthood:* the age at which we can reproduce.
- *Legal adulthood:* the age at which the law says we can vote, purchase alcohol, get a driver's licence, marry etc. Note, however, that these definitions do not produce an unequivocal answer. The trappings of adult status are attained at varying and differing ages in different cultures.
- *Social adulthood:* the age at which we start performing adult roles, such as the role of full-time worker, spouse, parent, voting citizen etc. Again, these do not coalesce around a single point in time.
- *Psychological adulthood:* the age at which we arrive at a self-concept of being responsible for our own lives, of being self-directing.

Alan Rogers (1996: 35), dissatisfied with attempts to generate a concise and satisfactory definition of an adult, came up instead with three clusters of ideas that 'lie within any view of adulthood':

- Some notion of being *fully grown* – or at least of having reached a certain level on the path to *maturity* or *full development.* This includes not only Knowles' biological definition of adulthood as sexual maturity, but also the notion of personal growth, the expansion and utilisation of all the individuals' talents, and the process of moving towards still greater maturity.
- A *sense of perspective*, best illustrated by comparing it to what we deem to be childishness:

    There are occasions when an older person is regarded as behaving 'childishly', in a non-adult fashion. Such childishness may consist of the individual seeing themselves as either being more important than they are seen by others to be, or conversely, as less important than they really are. The former throws a tantrum, acts petulantly, makes a fuss and is frequently further infuriated by the accusation of childish behaviour;

the latter withdraws, sulks or submits passively, normally accepting the charge of childishness with less hostility. In both cases we expect 'adults' to behave with a greater sense of *perspective* than is being shown, a perspective that will lead to sounder judgements about themselves and about others. We expect them to have accumulated experience that, if drawn upon, will help them achieve a more balanced approach to life and to society. (Rogers, 1996: 35–6)

■ *Self-responsibility* – being responsible for oneself, for one's own deeds and one's own development.

Although we often think of adulthood in terms of chronological age, it is a process rather than a status, and the criteria of adulthood are attained gradually. The process of developing a sense of self-directedness can start early in life, and grow cumulatively as we become biologically mature, start performing adult-like roles and take increasing responsibility for our own decisions. We become adult by degrees, and having a fully fledged sense of ourself as self-directed probably does not occur until we have achieved, or consciously rejected, several normative trappings of adulthood, such as leaving full-time education, having a full-time job, being in a settled relationship and having children. No adult is ever likely to have fulfilled all criteria that could denote adulthood, but, given the emphasis on chronological age as a convenient marker of appropriate developmental status, it is unsurprising that people – both counsellors and clients – are often concerned about 'How well am I doing for my age?'

Activity 3: Life chapters

By beginning to explore your own life course, this third exercise in the Activity Trail gives, in a small way, testimony to your own experience – the route that brought you to where you are today.

The exercise can be completed in many different ways and, because of this, it can be valuable to discuss your 'Life chapters' with one or more colleagues, and compare the different ways you have approached this task. Activity 11: Exploring your story, builds on the current activity by fleshing out the content of these chapters in far greater detail.

Despite individual variations, it is quite probable that your Life chapters are in some way anchored to chronological age; although it is rarely age *per se* that defines a chapter or the transition from one chapter to the next. Rather, the focus of particular chapters often revolves around different roles to do with education, work or personal life – being a pre-schooler, at primary school, unemployed, working in a particular job, being married, being single, being divorced etc. The beginning and end of chapters are frequently marked by discontinuities or significant redirections in your life – role entry or exit, perhaps, or a major loss, or some other significant life event. Whereas a focus on life *stages* tends to direct attention to chronological age or shared normative transitions, a focus on life *chapters* allows you to find and identify the unique 'natural breaks' in your life course. Think about the extent to which your 'natural breaks' conform to social norms. To what extent do they reflect an alternating sequence of structure-changing and structure-building phases?

Think about the overall tenor of your 'Table of Contents'. What does it mainly depict – change or continuity? Is it very much about you and you alone, or is it more about your relationships with people, places and organisations? What do the chapters predominantly reflect – your main activities at the time, your key relationships, or your inner being?

Activity 4: Developmental stages and tasks

The first task in this activity – 'Where would you place the boundaries between stages?' – relates to the question of what constitutes a life stage. Take a moment to consider the length of the various stages that you have identified. I find only rarely that they are all of approximately the same chronological length (for example, 'under '10', '10 to 19', 'the 20s', 'the 30s' etc.). More generally, the stages are of widely differing length – often with many stages crowded into the years of infancy, childhood and adolescence, and then great swathes of time allocated to a single phase during the adult years. This generally reflects the dramatic impact of physical and cognitive development during the earlier years of life and the personal and social changes that they provoke, in comparison to the less tangible and more socially constructed phases of adulthood.

The remaining questions in Activity 4 are directly related to the topic of developmental tasks. Think about the origins of the tasks you identified – what is the ratio for different tasks of the three sources identified by Robert Havighurst (1972): physical maturation, social norms and personal aspirations?

Havighurst developed lists of six to nine developmental tasks for each of six life stages, amending the lists throughout his career as social changes made some of them obsolete or outdated. Describing the tasks in fairly general terms (for example, 'Exploring intimate relationships' rather than 'Learning to live with a marriage partner') can render them less susceptible to changing social norms, as in the list below, which has been adapted from Newman and Newman's (1995) attempt to identify the major issues that dominate a person's learning and problem-solving efforts during a given stage.

Life stage	Developmental tasks
Infancy (birth to 2 years)	Social attachment
	Development of the senses
	Motor development, leading to walking
	Learning through sensory and motor interactions with the environment
	Understanding the nature of objects and the creation of categories
	Emotional development
Early childhood	
(i) Toddlerhood (2–4 years)	Developing mobility and other physical skills
	Fantasy play

	Language development Development of self-control
(ii) Early school age (4–6 years)	Sex-role identification Early moral development Self-theory Conceptual skills Group play
Middle childhood (6–12 years)	Friendship Development of concrete thinking Skill learning Self-evaluation Team play
Adolescence (12–18 years)	Physical maturation Development of abstract reasoning Personal ideology Emotional development Membership in the peer group Sexual relationships
Early adulthood	
(i) Fledging adulthood (18–25 years)	Autonomy from parents Gender identity Internalised morality Career choice
(ii) Young adulthood (25–40 years)	Exploring intimate relationships Childbearing and rearing Work Lifestyle
Middle adulthood (40–65 years)	Management of career Renegotiating the couple relationship Expanding caring relationships Management of the household Adjusting to ageing parents Coping with physical changes of ageing
Late adulthood	
(i) Early late-adulthood (65–75 years)	Promotion of intellectual vigour Redirection of energy towards new roles and activities Acceptance of one's life Development of a point of view about death
(ii) Late late-adulthood (75 years onwards)	Coping with physical changes of ageing Development of a psychohistorical perspective Facing the unknown

How similar is this list to the one you generated? To what extent does it reflect developmental tasks in other than a Western, post-industrial society? To what extent do you see these tasks reflected in the issues that clients of different ages bring to counselling? Do you find the idea of developmental tasks helpful, or do you find it confining – smothering the uniqueness of each individual life?

Activity 5: Lifeline

The Lifeline exercise exists in many versions and it could also be thought of as a graphical version of Activity 3: Life chapters. It has the advantage of suggesting in visual form both the eventfulness of a life (indicated by the number of 'peaks' and 'troughs' punctuating the line) and the degree of dramatic tension (expressed by the steepness of the upward and downward slopes) (Gergen, 1988).

Over the last two decades I have asked hundreds of students (of counselling or otherwise) to complete this exercise. It is rare that it does not trigger much food for thought – both personal and academic. I never cease to be fascinated by the myriad ways in which people tackle the exercise and make it relevant to their own situation and need. Sometimes it is completed systematically, with chronological age marked in equally sized intervals along the horizontal line. More often, though, it is completed less precisely, with periods of upheaval and change receiving most attention, sometimes with several years of greater tranquillity being passed over in a mere centimetre or two. It is not unusual for people to be unwilling or unable to project their Lifeline into the future. Most do have a go, however – although these projections are generally quite vague and unspecific (sometimes drawn more faintly or as a dotted line, as if to indicate lack of certainty), and often reflecting hopes rather than necessarily expectations. Often the Lifeline is punctuated by sudden changes of direction and by dramatic highs and lows. When, however, the whole line is relatively flat, its author rarely claims this is because it depicts an uneventful or emotionally neutral life. Rather, it tends to be because the author found it hard to sum up a multifaceted and multi-directional life course within a single line – any one moment can be, to use the opening words of Dickens' (1994) *Tale of Two Cities*, both 'the best of times' and 'the worst of times'. Indeed, one development of the activity is to draw several lifelines representing, for example, Gilmore's (1973) three domains of work (or endeavour), relationships and aloneness (or self). The similarities and differences in their shape and rhythm can then be explored, along with points in time when the trajectory of one line influenced or was influenced by the trajectory of another. However, to do all this is very time-consuming, and most people – even if they are primarily aware of its limitations – are able to produce some sort of a Lifeline that they can use as a basis for reflecting on their own life course (past, present and future) and, on the waxing and waning of recurrent themes and preoccupations.

The questions following the completion of the lifeline in Activity 5 are designed to lead you into discussion of several issues related to the study of the life course, including: the balance between losses and gains; the criteria against which we judge the quality of our life; the triggers of transitions; and the possibility of post-traumatic growth. Your lifeline is a representation of your life course that you might return to as different topics are raised in subsequent chapters of the book.

Activity 6: Curriculum vitae

The curriculum vitae asked for in this activity is not, I suspect, quite the one you would prepare for a job application. It is, perhaps, more like one you might put together during a career planning workshop, where the aim is not to market yourself to a potential employer, but to engage in exploration and decision making about your career goals and aspirations.

The aim of the activity is to provide you with a basis for considering how your professional self has evolved since you made the decision to embark on training in counselling. Think about your responses in relation to the career stages identified by Donald Super et al. (1988). Can you place yourself on the sequence of exploration; establishment; maintenance; and disengagement? Perhaps your experience resonates more with Skovholt and Ronnestad's (1995) account of the stages of professional counsellor development. Do you, then, see professional development as growth towards professional individuation?

Activity 7: Working with clients of different ages

We see ourselves and others through a filter of age, but since this filter can be distorting, it is important that it is examined so that its impact can be acknowledged and better understood. It is towards this end that the present activity is directed. Issues concerning working with clients of different ages emerge throughout the chapter of which this activity is a part. Also relevant are the discussion of age and ageism, in Chapter 1 and the summary, in Chapter 6, of key issues on which the client's age has an impact. These issues include:

- the social and economic power that is typically associated with different life stages;
- the cognitive and physical standing of the client;
- the implications of being a member of a particular cohort or generation;
- the client's reaction to the counsellor's age and life stage;
- the counsellor's reaction to the client's age and life stage; and
- the significance of all of the above for the development of empathy.

Sometimes I find that people are uncomfortable with this exercise when it is first presented to them. The usual objection is along the lines of 'It's the person that I see, not their age' – a comment that suggests an implicit awareness that chronological age is nothing more than an indicator of the amount of time that has passed since birth, and that time, *per se,* causes nothing. In this sense it is right to be age-blind, and to rail against pervasive and deeply embedded networks of age-related norms and expectations. On reflection, however, most people conclude that age is a significant, albeit often unacknowledged, dimension in the counselling relationship. The time we have lived has not been a vacuum: 'Years are not empty containers', writes Andrews (1999: 309); 'important things happen in that time. Why must these years be trivialised? They are the stuff of which people's lives are made'. And it is this 'stuff' that clients bring to counselling. To cut ourselves off from our age is to cut ourselves off from part of who we are.

I have used this activity primarily with counsellors in training who have only recently begun their practice. They have therefore only limited experience of working with clients, and have certainly not worked with clients over a wide age range. They can, however, draw on their own personal experience in addressing this task. There is often recognition that their own family situation has an impact. If they have lived through the rebellions of their adolescent children, if they have cared for frail elderly parents, if they have weathered the storms of divorce or bereavement, then there is often a feeling that this makes them better able to work with clients facing similar issues. If they are currently in the midst of such life events, then they recognise the difficulty they may have in sufficiently disentangling themselves from their own experience. The activity can, therefore, also lead into discussion of fitness to practise.

Ironically, bringing the issue of a client's age to the foreground in this activity can reduce its power. Its impact becomes less hidden and subversive. Age is more than a mask (Featherstone and Hepworth, 1989, 1990). But it is not all-determining. By acknowledging and bringing into the open the significance of age it then becomes easier to look beyond the mask of age to the agelessness as well as the ageing of the person beneath.

Activity 8: Transitions and turning points

My experience has been that the first task in this exercise – generating the list of major landmarks in your life – represents the hub of the activity, and is far from the simple task that it might first appear. I have never used this exercise with children, but I find that young adults under the age of about 22 or 23 ('fledgling adults' in the terminology used in Chapter 3) not infrequently find it difficult to generate a list of more than 10 or so significant landmarks in their life. Older respondents rarely have this problem, but are often surprised both by what they end up including in their list, and by what they leave out. Often it is only during the discussion stage of the activity that people become aware of the 'big events' that they have left off their list. This underscores vividly the significance of the meaning and interpretation of an event over its objective, tangible characteristics.

The questions in this activity about 'types' of events and their timing relates to some of the conceptual distinctions used in discussing the life course. One distinction is between normative age-graded, normative history-graded and non-normative events (Baltes et al., 1980).

- *Normative age-graded events* are biologically and environmentally determined events that have a fairly strong relationship with chronological age. Learning to walk is an example of the former, and the age at which we enter the education system is, within any particular society, an example of the latter. Often these events are shared by many members of a particular society, but there may be some rarely occurring events (such as the onset of a particular illness) that are nonetheless associated with a particular chronological age.
- *Normative history-graded events* are events that have a fairly strong relationship with historical time rather than chronological age. They are cohort specific, being shared by members of a particular generation, but not – or not in the same way – by members of the generations preceding or following them.
- *Non-normative events* are the events that occur more or less randomly with regard to age or life stage. They are the events that might happen to us at any age, and are not necessarily ones that are shared by others of our generation.

Age-graded normative events make up a significant part of the normal, expectable life cycle, and it has been suggested (Neugarten, 1979) that such events tend to pose fewer difficulties of adaptation than do those events that are unexpected or 'off time'. However, sometimes the fact that the events were anticipated, along with the sense that most other people seem to be coping fine, can accentuate feelings of inadequacy if we struggle – especially if the event had long been a part of our life plan and had, indeed, been anticipated with pleasure. When we achieve the job of our dreams; the perfect home; the much-longed-for child etc., any difficulties of adjustment we might have can be accentuated by the sense that 'I shouldn't feel this way – I've got exactly what I wanted'.

If you found that the life events in your list clustered around particular points in the life course, then think about whether this reflects Levinson et al.'s (1978) distinction between structure-changing and structure-building phases of the life course. This might be the moment to return to the discussion of Levinson's concept of the evolving life structure that was introduced in Chapter 1.

Overall, this activity is a validity check on the models and concepts introduced in Chapter 4, introducing readers in a concrete rather than an abstract way to issues such as those raised by the following questions.

- What do we mean by a transition or turning point?
- What makes a life event 'significant'?
- How might our passage through transitions be helped, or hindered?

This activity can also usefully be examined in the context of Activity 3: Life chapters and Activity 5: Lifeline. Do, for example, the landmark events chosen in this activity correspond to some of the events marking the beginning or end of chapters in Activity 3, or the peaks or troughs in Activity 5?

Activity 9: Stability zones

Counselling is inextricably entwined with making changes – of behaviour, thoughts, feelings, awareness, understandings, interpretations. Tumults and upheavals cry out and grab our attention, making it all too easy to overlook that which might, by remaining constant, hold us steady. But this is what a stability zone does. Like the light in T.S. Eliot's (1944) *Burnt Norton* it is a 'still point in the turning world'.

Because of their reliability and constancy it is easy to overlook stability zones, or take them for granted until we need them – at which point we may discover that they are in fact less permanent or effective than we had assumed. Both our stability zones and what we need of them change over time, and it is important, therefore, that they are recognised, nurtured and developed. The next activity trail exercise – Activity 10: Interpersonal support convoys – explores 'people' stability zones. An activity that can foster awareness of 'things' as stability zones is the values clarification exercise *Saved From the Fire*. This is what you do.

- Imagine that your house is on fire. All occupants – people and animals – are safe, and you have the chance to save 10 items from the blaze.
- Think about, and then list, the 10 items that you would choose.
- Share your list with another person or a small group, saying something about the reasons for your choice. If possible, bring one of the most important (and most portable) items along with you.

Reflect on what the items on your list mean to you. Sometimes the items selected are of practical value or importance – home insurance details, passport, financial documents – and sometimes they are of high monetary value or intrinsic beauty. More often, however, the value of the items chosen is primarily symbolic. Things can be stability zones not only in and of themselves, but also as links with other stability zones and reminders of who we are and what we have been.

Activity 10: Interpersonal support convoys

An interpersonal support convoy is a particular type of stability zone that focuses on personal relationships. What the idea of a convoy captures particularly well is the dynamic nature of stability zones – whilst offering stability, they are not static. Figuratively, an interpersonal support convoy would be better represented as a series of concentric tubes rather than circles, with some members of the convoy moving, over time, between rings – some moving towards the core, whilst others gravitate towards the outer rings and perhaps leave the convoy altogether.

A point to consider is whether, when a person near the centre of our convoy dies, do they disappear from our convoy altogether? Literally, of course they do – their physical and breathing presence has gone. But figuratively, they may remain – 'I wonder what Jim would have advised', we might ask ourself; 'Mary would have been pleased to see me do that', we might say. In this way, the bonds between ourself and the person who has died can continue, as discussed in the section in Chapter 5 on transitions. As the bonds are reformulated to accommodate the physical absence of the deceased, the relationship moves from being a stability zones in the 'people' category towards being an example of an 'ideas' stability zone.

It is worth reflecting for a moment on the placement of a counselling relationship in the client's support convoy. The relationship is actually a professional, role-dependent relationship, although its relational depth may lend it some of the quality of a relationship that is more typically nearer the centre of the convoy. This is one of the factors that makes boundary and dual-role issues, as well as the management of endings, so important in counselling. If a counselling relationship is suddenly or insensitively severed, the client can feel bereft – feeling as if they have lost a friendship rather than a professional service. Similarly, trainee counsellors have to learn how to handle feelings of abandonment and rejection when clients either do not show up for their appointments, or prematurely (in the counsellor's view) terminate their counselling.

Activity 11: Exploring your story

Dan McAdams proposes that in contemporary society, psychotherapy and autobiography are the two most common tools through which we identify our personal narrative. Many counsellors will have experienced the former. Activity 11 provides one structure for attempting the latter as well. The commentary below makes reference to the key structural elements of a life story that are summarised in Chapter 5 in the section on 'story as identity'. It will make greater sense if you have read this section of the book before tackling the commentary.

- **Life chapters.** From Activity 3: Life chapters (in Chapter 2), you may already have found a way of organising your personal narrative that both reminds you and enhances your understanding of the major landmarks and developmental trends in your life. In terms of narrative elements, completion of the life chapters exercise is likely to give indications of both narrative tone and personal imagery.
- **Key event.** Supplementary prompts and questions (McAdams, 1997) for exploring key events in your personal narrative include the following.

What happened?
Where was I?
Who was involved?
What did I do?
What was I thinking and feeling at the time?
What impact has this event had on my life story?
What does it say about who I am or was?
Did the event change me in any way? If so, how?

Analysis of key events should generate further insight into narrative tone and personal imagery. It may also be possible to begin to distinguish the role of different motivational themes.

- **Significant people.** This section of the interview, not surprisingly, generates information about the characters (or imagoes) that populate our narrative. McAdams suggests that the people selected might include, but not necessarily be limited to, your parents, children, siblings, spouses, lovers, friends, teachers, colleagues and mentors. He advocates choosing at least one person to whom you are not related. You might also think about including in your choice a particular hero or heroine – either real or fictitious – who has been important to you.
- **Future script.** This section switches attention from the past to the future. Our plans and goals – and, notably, our dreams for the future – reflect our basic needs and wants and, as with key events, are likely to reveal the motivational themes in our life story. McAdams suggests a particular prompt for this section, namely:

  How, if at all, does your dream, plan or outline for the future enable you to (1) be creative and (2) make a contribution to others.

  This question addresses your approach to generativity – the creation of a gift of the self that is offered to the next generation.
- **Stresses and problems.** It is likely that you have already touched on some areas of difficulty in your life. This section provides the opportunity to consider the nature of the stress, problem or conflict in some detail. Outline the source of the concern, how it developed, and your plan, if you have one, for dealing with it in the future.

  This analysis can signal issues and conflicts that may need to be resolved in successive revisions of the personal narrative – perhaps, for example, allowing valued but hitherto underdeveloped characters or imagoes to flourish.
- **Personal ideology.** Questions in this section relate to the ideological setting of your life story; your fundamental beliefs and values, such as:

  any belief you might have in the existence of some kind of god, deity, or force that in some way influences or organises the universe;
  the essence of any such beliefs, and the ways, if any, in which your beliefs differ from those of most people you know;
  ways in which your religious beliefs have changed over time;

your political position;
what you consider to be the most important value in human living.

■ **Overall life theme**. This final section provides an explicit opportunity, at the end of what might have been a lengthy period of reflection, to consider the overall meaning of your personal narrative. It is not, however, an endpoint, as McAdams (1997: 264) makes clear:

> Identifying your personal myth should be seen as a life process. It cannot be fully achieved in a single interview. The questions I have posed should get you going. But don't stop with my questions. Plan to meet with your listener again. Follow up on interesting leads of the first interview. Make time to get to know yourself and to share yourself with the listener. The process is enjoyable in itself. And it promises to pay personal dividends in enhancing your understanding of the story you live by.

In her book, *Introducing Narrative Psychology*, Michele Crossley (2000) gives detailed and very specific guidelines for exploring and analysing your own personal narrative using the schedule designed by Dan McAdams. She includes an extended extract from an interview in which she acted as listener for a 21-year-old male student, and then draws on this material in her account of how to analyse autobiographical interviews. It would be well worth looking at Crossley's discussion if you plan to give a lot of time and attention to this activity. Alternatively, detailed suggestions, guidance and encouragement can be found in Tristine Rainer's (1998) *Your Life as Story*.

Activity 12: Biographical interviewing

This activity represents another way of accessing life stories. Its guidelines are less specific than are those for Activity 11: Exploring your story, and it directed at biography rather than autobiography – you are the listener/interviewer rather than the speaker/interviewee.

For many years I have used biographical interviewing as a basis for student assignments. It allows for a reflexive approach to the evaluation of concepts and models of the life course, and also provides a vehicle for considering a number of issues relevant to counselling practice and ethics. After completing a biographical interview, bring your thoughts together by addressing the following questions.

■ To what extent did the person's story demonstrate the stages or dynamics of the models discussed in this text?
■ How did the interviewee tell their story? What type of story was it? What themes were covered?
■ How did the client's age and life stage *vis-à-vis* my own age and life stage affect the interview and what did I learn from it?
■ How did various theoretical models and concepts help me understand this person?

- How did this person help me understand the theoretical models and concepts?
- How might the issues addressed in this activity, and in this book as a whole, inform my work as a counsellor?

As already noted, a biographical interview is both similar to and different from counselling, and this exercise provides a vehicle for considering their overlaps and their distinctions. In so doing, understanding of the nature of counselling can be enhanced. A key difference between the two is that, in this activity it is, in effect, you who is the key client. Whilst parts of the interview might well be conducted as if the interviewee were the client, if you were not carrying out this exercise, the interview would not be taking place. The interview is, therefore, being conducted primarily for your bene-fit with the interviewee assisting you, rather than vice versa. You might like to consider how this affects the way you conducted the interview. If your interviewee had been a client, and if the interview had been a counselling session, would your way of working have been very different? Are there top-ics you would have pursued in greater depth? Are there boundary issues that you might have handled differently?

The fact that you are the main beneficiary of the exercise does not, how-ever, mean that the interviewee gains nothing. Generally both interviewees and interviewers find the experience surprisingly rewarding – indicative, perhaps, of how in our daily life we do not often have the opportunity to explore and share our life story with an interested listener.

References

Ainscow, M. (2000). *Welcome address*. Paper presented at the BAC: Sixth Annual Counselling Research Conference, University of Manchester.

Andrews, M. (1999). The seductiveness of agelessness. *Aging and Society, 19*, 301–18.

Antonucci, T.C. (1991). Attachment, social support, and coping with negative life events in mature adulthood. In E.M. Cummings, A.L. Greene and K.H. Kramer (eds), *Life-span Developmental Psychology: Perspectives on Stress and Coping*. Hillsdale, NJ: Lawrence Erlbaum.

Apter, T. (2001). *The Myth of Maturity*. London: Norton.

Apter, T. (2002). The myth of maturity. *Association for University and College Counselling Journal, Special issue*, November, pp. 2–7.

Arnett, J.J. (1999). Adolescent storm and stress reconsidered. *American Psychologist, 54*, 317–26.

Arnett, J.J. (2000). Emerging adulthood: a theory of development from the late teens through the twenties. *American Psychologist, 55*, 469–80.

Baltes, P.B. (1987). Theoretical propositions of life-span developmental psychology. *Developmental Psychology, 23*, 611–26.

Baltes, P.B., Reese, H.W., and Lipsitt, L.P. (1980). Life-span developmental psychology. *Annual Review of Psychology, 31*, 65–110.

Bateson, M.C. (1990). *Composing a Life*. New York: Plenum.

Bee, H. (1994). *Lifespan Development*. New York: HarperCollins.

Berne, E. (1975). *What Do You Say After You Say Hello? The Psychology of Human Destiny*. London: Corgi.

Biggs, S. (1999). *The Mature Imagination: Dynamics of Identity in Midlife and Beyond*. Buckingham: Open University Press.

Biggs, S. (2003). Counselling psychology and midlife issues. In R. Woolfe, W. Dryden and S. Strawbridge (eds), *Handbook of Counselling Psychology* (2nd edn). London: Sage.

Blocher, D. (2000). *Counseling: A Developmental Approach* (4th edn). Chichester: John Wiley.

Borden, W. (1989). Life review as a therapeutic frame in the treatment of young adults with AIDS. *Health and Social Work, 14*, 253–9.

Bowlby, J. (1980). *Attachment and Loss. Volume 3. Loss: Sadness and Depression*. London: Hogarth.

Bridges, W. (1980). *Transitions: Making Sense of Life's Changes*. New York: Addison-Wesley.

British Association for Counselling and Psychotherapy (2002). *Ethical Framework for Good Practice in Counselling and Psychotherapy*. Rugby: BACP.

Bronfenbrenner, U. (1979). *The Ecology of Human Development*. Cambridge, MA: Harvard University Press.

Bronfenbrenner, U. (1992). Ecological systems theory. In R. Vasta (ed.), *Six Theories of Child Development: Revised Formulations and Current Issues*. London: Jessica Kingsley.

Brown, P., and Smith, A.A. (1996). Psychological counselling in mid-life issues. In R. Woolfe and W. Dryden (eds), *Handbook of Counselling Psychology*. London: Sage.

Buchanan, C.M., Eccles, J.S., Flanagan, C., Midgley, C., Fledlaufer, H., and Harold, R.D. (1990). Parents' and teachers' beliefs about adolescents: effects of sex and experience. *Journal of Youth and Adolescence, 19*, 363–94.

Butler, R.N. (1963). The life review: an interpretation of reminiscence in the aged. *Psychiatry, 26*, 65–76.

Butler, R.N. (1969). Age-ism: another form of bigotry. *The Gerontologist, 9*, 243–6.

Cannon, W.B. (1939). *The Wisdom of the Body*. New York: Norton.

Carlsen, M. (1988). *Meaning Making: Therapeutic Process in Adult Development*. New York: Norton.

Chaplin, J. (1988). Feminist therapy. In J. Rowan and W. Dryden (eds), *Innovative Therapy in Britain*. Buckingham: Open University Press.

Chickering, A.W., and Havighurst, R.J. (1981). The life cycle. In A. Chickering and associates (eds), *The Modern American College: Responding to the New Realities of Diverse Students and a Changing Society*. San Francisco, CA: Jossey-Bass.

Cochran, L. (1997). *Career Counselling: A Narrative Approach*. Thousand Oaks, CA: Sage.

Cohler, B.J. (1982). Personal narrative and the life course. In P.B. Baltes and O.G. Brim (eds), *Life-span Development and Behavior*. New York: Academic Press.

Coles, S. (1996). Counselling in occupational therapy. In S. Palmer, S. Dainow and P. Milner (eds), *Counselling: The BAC Counselling Reader*. London: Sage.

Cooper, C. (1996). Psychological counselling with young adults. In R. Woolfe and W. Dryden (eds), *Handbook of Counselling Psychology*. London: Sage.

Cooper, C. (2003). Psychological counselling with young adults. In R. Woolfe, W. Dryden and S. Strawbridge (eds), *Handbook of Counselling Psychology* (2nd edn). London: Sage.

Crompton, M. (1992). *Children and Counselling*. London: Edward Arnold.

Crossley, M.L. (2000). *Introducing Narrative Psychology: Self, Trauma and the Construction of Meaning*. Buckingham: Open University Press.

Cumming, E. (1975). Engagement with an old theory. *International Journal of Aging and Human Development, 6*, 187–91.

Cumming, E., and Henry, W. (1961). *Growing Old: The Process of Disengagement*. New York: Basic Books.

Cupitt, D. (1997). *After God: The Future of Religion*. London: Phoenix.

Dan, A.J., and Bernhard, L.A. (1989). Menopause and other health issues for midlife women. In S. Hunter and M. Sundel (eds), *Midlife Myths: Issues, Findings and Practice Implications*. Newbury Park, CA: Sage.

Davey, B. (2001). The life-course perspective. In B. Davey (ed.), *Birth to Old Age: Health in Transition* (2nd edn). Buckingham: Open University Press.

Dickens, C. (1994). *A Tale of Two Cities*. London: Penguin Popular Classics. (First published in 1859.)

Downey, J. (1996). Psychological counselling of children and young people. In R. Woolfe and W. Dryden (eds), *Handbook of Counselling Psychology*. London: Sage.

Downey, J. (2003). Psychological counselling of children and young people. In W. Dryden, R. Woolfe and S. Strawbridge (eds), *Handbook of Counselling Psychology* (2nd edn). London: Sage.

Dryden, W., and Spurling, L. (eds). (1989). *Becoming a Psychotherapist*. London: Tavistock/Routledge.

Egan, G. (1990). *The Skilled Helper: A Systematic Approach to Effective Helping* (4th edn). Monterey, CA: Brooks/Cole.

Eliot, T.S. (1944). *Burnt Norton*. In T.S. Eliot, *The Four Quartets*. London: Faber.

Erikson, E.H. (1980). *Identity and the Life Cycle: A Reissue*. New York: Norton.

Fear, R., and Woolfe, R. (1999). The personal and professional development of the counsellor: the relationship between personal philosophy and theoretical orientation. *Counselling Psychology Quarterly, 12*, 253–62.

Featherstone, M., and Hepworth, M. (1989). Ageing and old age: reflections on the postmodern life course. In B. Bytheway, T. Keil, P. Allatt and A. Bryman (eds), *Becoming and Being Old: Sociological Approaches to Later Life*. London: Sage.

Featherstone, M., and Hepworth, M. (1990). Images of ageing. In J. Bond and P. Coleman (eds), *Ageing in Society*. London: Sage.

Fisher, S., and Cooper, C.L. (eds). (1990). *On the Move: The Psychology of Change and Transition*. Chichester: John Wiley.

Freud, S. (1955). Beyond the pleasure principle. In J. Strachey (ed.) The Standard Edition of the Complete Psychological Works of Sigmund Freud (Volume 18). London: Hogarth.

Friedman, W.J. (1993). Memory for the time of past events. *Psychological Bulletin, 113*, 44–66.

Garland, J. (1994). What splendour, it all coheres: life-review therapy with older people. In J. Bornat (ed.), *Reminiscence Reviewed: Perspectives, Evaluation, Achievements*. Buckingham: Open University Press.

Geertjens, L., and Waaldijk, O. (1998). Client-centred therapy for adolescents: an interactional point of view. In B. Thorne and E. Lambers (eds), *Person-centred Therapy: A European Perspective*. London: Sage.

Geldard, K., and Geldard, D. (1999). *Counselling Adolescents*. London: Sage.

Gergen, M.M. (1988). Narrative structures in social explanation. In C. Antaki (ed.), *Analysing Everyday Explanation: A Casebook of Methods*. London: Sage.

Gilmore, S.K. (1973). *The Counselor-in-training*. Englewood Cliffs, NJ: Prentice-Hall.

Goldfried, M.R. (2001a). Conclusion: a perspective on how therapists change. In M.R. Goldfried (ed.), *How Therapists Change: Personal and Professional Reflections*. Washington, DC: American Psychological Association.

Goldfried, M.R. (ed.). (2001b). *How Therapists Change: Personal and Professional Reflections*. Washington, DC: American Psychological Association.

Goudie, F. (2003). Psychological therapy with older adults. In R. Woolfe, W. Dryden and S. Strawbridge (eds), *Handbook of Counselling Psychology* (2nd edn). London: Sage.

Greenberg, L.S. (2001). My change process: from certainty through chaos to complexity. In M.R. Goldfried (ed.), *How Therapists Change: Personal and Professional Reflections*. Washington, DC: American Psychological Association.

Gustafson, J.P. (1992). *Self-delight in a Harsh World: The Main Stories of Individual, Marital and Family Psychotherapy*. New York: Norton.

Haraven, T.K., and Adams, K.J. (eds). (1982). *Ageing and Life Course Transitions: An Interdisciplinary Perspective*. London: Tavistock.

Havighurst, R.J. (1972). *Developmental Tasks and Education* (3rd edn). New York: David McKay. (First edition, 1948.)

Havighurst, R.J., Neugarten, B.L., and Tobin, S.S. (1968). Disengagement and patterns of aging. In B.L. Neugarten (ed.), *Middle Age and Aging*. Chicago: University of Chicago Press.

Heckhausen, J. (1999). *Developmental Regulation in Adulthood: Age-normative and Sociostructural Constraints as Adaptive Challenges*. Cambridge: Cambridge University Press.

Heckhausen, J. (2001). Adaptation and resilience in midlife. In M.E. Lachman (ed.), *Handbook of Midlife Development*. New York: John Wiley.

Heckhausen, J., and Lang, F.R. (1996). Social construction and old age: normative conceptions and interpersonal processes. In G.R. Semin and K. Fiedler (eds), *Applied Social Psychology*. London: Sage.

Hopson, B. (1981). Response to the papers by Schlossberg, Brammer and Abrego. *Counseling Psychologist*, 9, 36–9.

Hopson, B., and Adams, J. (1976). Towards an understanding of transition: defining some boundaries of transition dynamics. In J. Adams, J. Hayes and B. Hopson (eds), *Transition: Understanding and Managing Personal Change*. London: Martin Robertson.

Houts, A.C., Shutty, M.S., and Emery, R.E. (1985). The impact of children on adults. In B. Lahey and A. Kazdin (eds), *Advances in Clinical Child Psychology, Volume 8*. New York: Plenum Press.

Howard, G.S. (1991). Culture tales: a narrative approach to thinking, cross-cultural psychology and psychotherapy. *American Psychologist*, 46, 187–97.

Hunter, S., and Sundel, M. (eds). (1989). *Midlife Myths: Issues, Findings and Practice Implications*. Newbury Park, CA: Sage.

Huyuk, M., and Guttman, D. (1999). Developmental issues in psychotherapy with older men. In M. Duffy (ed.), *Handbook of Counselling and Psychotherapy with Older Adults*. New York: John Wiley.

Itzin, C. (1986). Ageism awareness training: a model for group work. In C. Phillipson, M. Bernard and P. Strang (eds), *Dependency and Interdependency in Old Age: Theoretical Perspectives and Policy Alternatives*. London: Croom Helm.

Jacobs, M. (1985). *The Presenting Past: An Introduction to Practical Psychodynamic Counselling*. Buckingham: Open University Press.

Jacobs, M. (1998). *The Presenting Past: The Core of Psychodynamic Counselling and Therapy*. Buckingham: Open University Press.

Jacobs, M. (2000). Psychotherapy in the United Kingdom: past, present and future. *British Journal of Guidance and Counselling*, 28, 451–66.

Jaques, E. (1965). Death and the mid-life crisis. *International Journal of Psychoanalysis*, 46, 502–14.

Jaques, E. (1980). The mid-life crisis. In S.I. Greenspan and G.H. Pollock (eds), *The Course of Life: Psychoanalytic Contributions Toward Understanding Personality Development. Volume 3: Adulthood and Aging*. Washington, DC: National Institute of Mental Health.

Johnson, J., and Bytheway, B. (1993). Ageism: concept and definition. In J. Johnson and R. Slater (eds), *Ageing and Later Life*. London: Sage.

Jung, C.G. (1972). The transcendent function. In H. Read, M. Fordham, G. Adler and W. McGuire (eds), *The Structure and Dynamics of the Psyche. Volume 8, The Collected Works of C.G. Jung* (2nd edn). London: Routledge and Kegan Paul.

Kahn, R.L., and Antonucci, T.C. (1980). Convoys over the life course: attachment, roles and social support. In P.B. Baltes and O.G. Brim (eds), *Life-span Development and Behavior, Volume 3*. New York: Academic Press.

Kaufman, S. (1986). *The Ageless Self: Sources of Meaning in Late Life*. New York: Meridian.

Killilea, M. (1976). Mutual help organizations: interpretations in the literature. In G. Caplan and M. Killilea (eds), *Support Systems and Mutual Help: Multidisciplinary Explorations*. New York: Grune and Stratton.

King, P. (1980). The life cycle as indicated by the nature of the transference of the middle-aged and elderly. *International Journal of Psychoanalysis, 61*, 153–60.

Klass, D., Silverman, P., and Nickman, S. (eds). (1996). *Continuing Bonds: New Understandings of Grief*. London: Taylor and Francis.

Knight, B.G. (1996). *Psychotherapy with Older Adults* (2nd edn). London: Sage.

Knowles, M. (1990). *The Adult Learner: A Neglected Species*. Houston, TX: Gulf.

Kolb, D. (1984). *Experiential Learning: Experience as the Source of Learning and Development*. Englewood Cliffs, NJ: Prentice-Hall.

Kubler-Ross, E. (1970). *On Death and Dying*. London: Tavistock.

Kurtz, L.F. (1997). *Self-help and Support Groups*. London: Sage.

Lazarus, A.A. (2001). From insight and reflection to action and clinical breadth. In M.R. Goldfried (ed.), *How Therapists Change: Personal and Professional Reflections*. Washington, DC: American Psychological Association.

Levinson, D.J. (1986). A conception of adult development. *American Psychologist, 42*, 3–13.

Levinson, D.J. (1990). A theory of life structure development in adulthood. In C.N. Alexander and E.J. Langer (eds), *Higher Stages of Human Development: Perspectives on Adult Growth*. New York: Oxford University Press.

Levinson, D.J. (1996). *The Seasons of a Woman's Life*. New York: Random House.

Levinson, D.J., Darrow, D.N., Klein, E.B., Levinson, M.H., and McKee, B. (1978). *The Seasons of a Man's Life*. New York: A.A. Knopf.

Lewis, M.I., and Butler, R.N. (1974). Life-review therapy: putting memories to work in individual and group psychotherapy. *Geriatrics, 29*, 165–73.

Mabey, J., and Sorensen, B. (1995). *Counselling for Young People*. Buckingham: Open University Press.

Martindale, B. (1989). Becoming dependent again: the fears of some elderly persons and their younger therapists. *Psychoanalytic Psychotherapy, 4*, 67–75.

McAdams, D.P. (1996). Narrating the self in adulthood. In J. Birren, G. Kenyon, J.-K. Ruth, J. Schroots and T. Svensson (eds), *Aging and Biography: Explorations in Adult Development*. New York: Springer.

McAdams, D.P. (1997). *Stories We Live By: Personal Myths and the Making of the Self*. New York: William Morrow.

McDevitt, C. (2000). *Welcome address*. Paper presented at the BAC: Sixth Annual Counselling Research Conference, University of Manchester.

McLeod, J. (1997). *Narrative and Psychotherapy*. London: Sage.

Murgatroyd, S., and Woolfe, R. (1982). *Coping with Crisis: Understanding and Helping People in Need*. London: Harper and Row.

Neimeyer, R.A. (ed.). (2001). *Meaning Reconstruction and the Experience of Loss*. Washington, DC: American Psychological Association.

Neugarten, B. (1979). Time, age, and the life cycle. *American Journal of Psychiatry, 136*(7), 887–94. (Reprinted in D.A. Neugarten (ed.). (1996) *The Meaning of Age: Selected Papers of Bernice L. Neugarten*. Chicago: Chicago University Press.)

Neugarten, B.L. (1968). *Middle Age and Aging: A Reader in Social Psychology*. Chicago, IL: University of Chicago Press.

Neugarten, B.L. (1982). *Age or Need? Public Policies for Older People*. Beverly Hills, CA: Sage.

Neugarten, B.L., and Hagestad, G.O. (1976). Age and the life course. In R.H. Binstock and E. Shanas (eds), *Handbook of Aging and the Social Sciences*. New York: Van Nostrand Reinhold.

Newman, B., and Newman, P. (1995). *Development Through Life: A Psychosocial Approach* (6th edn). Pacific Grove, CA: Brooks/Cole.

Nicholson, N., and West, M. (1988). *Managerial Job Change: Men and Women in Transition*. Cambridge: Cambridge University Press.

Nin, A. (1967). *The Diary of Anaïs Nin, Volumes 1–7*. New York: Harcourt, Brace and World.

Noller, P., Feeney, J.A., and Peterson, C. (2000). *Personal Relationships Across the Life Span*. Brighton: Psychology Press.

Norcross, J.C., and Guy, J.C. (1989). Ten therapists: the process of becoming and being. In W. Dryden and L. Spurling (eds), *On Becoming a Psychotherapist*. London: Tavistock/Routledge.

O'Leary, E. (1996). *Counselling Older Adults*. London: Chapman and Hall.

Palmer, S., and G. McMahon (eds). (1997). *Handbook of Counselling* (2nd edn). London: Routledge.

Pedler, M., Burgoyne, J., and Boydell, T. (2001). *A Manager's Guide to Self-development* (4th edn). London: McGraw-Hill Education.

Pilgrim, D. (1997). *Psychotherapy and Society*. London: Sage.

Prochaska, J.O., DiClemente, C.C., and Norcross, J. (1992). In search of how people change: application to addictive behaviors. *American Psychologist, 47*, 1102–14.

Proctor, B., and Inskipp, F. (1999). *Post-tribalism: a millennium gift for clients*. Paper presented at the BAC: Annual Training Conference, University of Warwick.

Rainer, T. (1998). *Your Life as Story: Discovering the 'New Autobiography' and Writing Memoir as Literature*. New York: Tarcher/Putnam.

Ray, R.E., and McFadden, S.H. (2001). The web and the quilt: alternatives to the heroic journey toward spiritual development. *Journal of Adult Development, 8*, 201–11.

Reese, H.W., and Smyer, M.A. (1983). The dimensionalization of life-events. In E.J. Callahan and K.A. McCluskey (eds), *Life-span Developmental Psychology: Nonnormative Life Events*. New York: Academic Press.

Rice, F.P. (2001). *Human Development: A Life-span Approach* (4th edn). Englewood Cliffs, NJ: Prentice-Hall.

Richards, D. (2001). The remains of the day: counselling older clients. *Counselling and Psychotherapy Journal, 12*, 10–14.

Rivers, I. (1997). Lesbian, gay and bisexual development: theory, research and social issues. *Journal of Community and Applied Social Psychology, 7*, 329–43.

Roberts, J. (1994). *Tales and Transformations: Stories in Families and Family therapy.* New York: Norton.

Roberts, K. (1977). The social conditions, consequences and limitations of careers guidance. *British Journal of Guidance and Counselling,* 5, 1–9.

Robinson, W.L. (1974). Conscious competency – the mark of a competent instructor. *Personnel Journal,* 53, 538–9.

Rogers, A. (1996). *Teaching Adults* (2nd edn). Buckingham: Open University Press.

Rogers, C.R. (1967). *On Becoming a Person: A Therapist's View of Psychotherapy.* London: Constable.

Rogers, C.R. (1980). *A Way of Being.* Boston, MA: Houghton Mifflin.

Rowan, J. (1994). The ten bull herding pictures as a paradigm of counsellor training. *Counselling Psychology Review,* 9, 13–18.

Runyan, W.M. (1978). The life course as a theoretical orientation: sequences of person–situation interactions. *Journal of Personality,* 46, 569–93.

Rutter, M. (1996). Transitions and turning points in developmental psychopathology: as applied to the age span between childhood and mid-adulthood. *International Journal of Behavioral Development,* 19, 603–26.

Rutter, M., Graham, P., Chadwick, F., and Yule, W. (1976). Adolescent turmoil: fact or fiction? *Journal of Child Psychiatry and Psychology,* 17, 35–56.

Ryan, T., and Walker, R. (1997). *Life Story Work: A Practical Guide to Helping Children Understand their Past.* London: British Association for Adoption and Fostering.

Sacks, O. (1985). *The Man who Mistook his Wife for a Hat.* London: Duckworth.

Salmon, P. (1985). *Living in Time: A New Look at Personal Development.* London: Dent.

Schlossberg, N.K. (1981). A model for analysing human adaptation to transition. *Counseling Psychologist,* 9, 2–18.

Schlossberg, N.K., Waters, E.B., and Goodman, J. (1995). *Counselling Adults in Transition: Linking Practice with Theory.* New York: Springer.

Schutz, R., and Heckhausen, J. (1996). A life span model of successful aging. *American Psychologist,* 51, 702–14.

Scrutton, S. (1989). *Counselling Older People: A Creative Response to Ageing.* London: Edward Arnold.

Seifert, K.L., Hoffnung, R.J., and Hoffnung, M. (2000). *Lifespan Development* (2nd edn). Boston, MA: Houghton Mifflin.

Shanahan, M.J., Hofer, S.M., and Miech, R.A. (2003). Planful competence, the life course, and aging: retrospect and prospect. In S.H. Zarit, L.I. Pearlin and K.W. Schaie (eds), *Personal Control in Social and Life Course Contexts.* New York: Springer.

Silva, J.A., and Leiderman, P.H. (1986). The life-span approach to individual therapy: an overview with case presentation. In P.B. Baltes, D.L. Featherman and R.M. Lerner (eds), *Life-span Development and Behavior, Volume 7.* Hillsdale, NJ: Lawrence Erlbaum.

Skovholt, T.M., and Ronnestad, M.H. (1995). *The Evolving Professional Self: Stages and Themes in Therapist and Counselor Development.* Chichester: John Wiley.

Speedy, J. (2000). *The story of three generations: an exploration of the changing professional attitudes, cultures and self-descriptions of a group of counselling educators and trainers.* Paper presented at the BAC: Sixth Annual Counselling Research Conference, University of Manchester.

Spence, D.P. (1987). *The Freudian Metaphor: Toward Paradigm Change in Psychoanalysis*. New York: Norton.

Spinelli, E. (2002). Paradise lost? *Counselling and Psychotherapy Journal, 13*, 15–19.

Sprung, G.M. (1989). Transferential issues in working with older adults. *Social Casework: The Journal of Contemporary Social Work, 70*, 597–602.

Stationery Office. (2001). *Population Trends 104*. London: HMSO.

Stewart, M.J. (1990). Expanding theoretical conceptualizations of self-help groups. *Social Science and Medicine, 31*, 1057–66.

Stoltenberg, C., and Delworth, U. (1987). *Supervising Counselors and Therapists: A Developmental Approach*. San Francisco, CA: Jossey-Bass.

Stricker, G. (2001). How I learned to abandon certainty and embrace change. In M.R. Goldfried (ed.), *How Therapists Change: Personal and Professional Reflections*. Washington, DC: American Psychological Association.

Stroebe, M., Gergen, M.M., Gergen, K.J., and Stroebe, W. (1992). Broken hearts or broken bonds: love and death in the historical perspective. *American Psychologist, 47*, 1205–12.

Stroebe, W., and Stroebe, M.E. (1987). *Bereavement and Health: The Psychological and Physical Consequences of Partner Loss*. Cambridge: Cambridge University Press.

Sugarman, L. (1985). Dilemmas of the childbearing decision. *Counselling, 51*, 3–8.

Sugarman, L. (2001). *Life-span Development: Frameworks, Accounts and Strategies*. Hove: Psychology Press.

Sugarman, L. (2003). The life course as meta-model for counselling psychologists. In R. Woolfe, W. Dryden and S. Strawbridge (eds), *Handbook of Counselling Psychology* (2nd edn). London: Sage.

Sugarman, L., and Woolfe, R. (1997). Piloting the stream: the life cycle and counselling. In S. Palmer and G. McMahon (eds), *Handbook of Counselling* (2nd edn). London: Routledge.

Super, D.E. (1957). *The Psychology of Careers*. New York: Harper and Row.

Super, D.E. (1980). A life-span, life–space approach to career development. *Journal of Vocational Behavior, 16*, 282–98.

Super, D.E. (1990). A life-span, life–space approach to career development. In D. Brown and L. Brooks and Associates (eds), *Career Choice and Development* (2nd edn). San Francisco, CA: Jossey-Bass.

Super, D.E., Thompson, A.S., Lindeman, R.H., Myers, R.A., and Jordaan, J.P. (1988). *Adult Career Concerns Inventory*. Palo Alto, CA: Consulting Psychologists Press.

Terkel, S. (1975). *Working: People Talk About What They Do All Day and How They Feel About What They Do*. London: Wildwood House.

Thomas, R.M. (1990). *Counseling and Life-span Development*. London: Sage.

Toffler, A. (1970). *Future Shock*. London: Pan.

Totton, N. (2000). *Psychotherapy and Politics*. London: Sage.

Troll, L.E. (1989). Myths of midlife intergenerational relationships. In S. Hunter and M. Sundel (eds), *Midlife Myths: Issues, Findings and Practice Implications*. Newbury Park, CA: Sage.

Twining, C. (1996). Psychological counselling with older adults. In R. Woolfe and W. Dryden (eds), *Handbook of Counselling Psychology*. London: Sage.

Vaughan, S.M., and Kinnier, R.T. (1996). Psychological effects of a life review intervention for persons with HIV disease. *Journal of Counseling and Development, 75*, 115–23.

Viney, L. (1993). *Life Stories: Personal Construct Therapy with the Elderly*. Chichester: John Wiley.

Viney, L.L., and Bousfield, L. (1991). Narrative analysis: a method of psychosocial research for AIDS-affected people. *Social Science and Medicine, 32*, 757–65.

Vgotsky, L. (1994). The problem of the environment. In R. Van der Veer and J. Valsiner (eds), *The Vgotsky Reader*. Oxford: Blackwell.

Walsh, F., and McGoldrick, M. (1988). Loss and the family life cycle. In C.J. Falicov (ed.), *Family Transitions: Continuity and Change over the Life Cycle*. New York: Guilford Press.

Walter, T. (1996). A new model of grief: bereavement and biography. *Mortality, 1*, 7–25.

Walter, T. (1999). *On Bereavement: The Culture of Grief*. Buckingham: Open University Press.

Weg, R.B. (1989). Sexuality/sensuality in the middle years. In S. Hunter and M. Sundel (eds), *Midlife Myths: Issues, Findings and Practice Implications*. Newbury Park, CA: Sage.

Woolfe, R. (1998). Therapists' attitudes towards working with older people. *Journal of Social Work Practice, 12*, 141–9.

Woolfe, R. (2001). The helping process. *The Psychologist, 14*, 347.

Woolfe, R., and Biggs, S. (1997). Counselling older adults: issues and awareness. *Counselling Psychology Quarterly, 10*, 189–95.

Woolfe, R., and Dryden, W. (eds). (1996). *Handbook of Counselling Psychology*. London: Sage.

Woolfe, R., Dryden, W., and Strawbridge, S. (eds). (2003). *Handbook of Counselling Psychology* (2nd edn). London: Sage.

Worden, J.W. (1983). *Grief Counselling and Grief Therapy*. London: Routledge.

Worden, J.W. (1995). *Grief Counselling and Grief Therapy* (2nd edn). London: Routledge.

Index

124 *Counselling and the Life Course*

biographical interviewing
    91–3, 112–13
biological adulthood 101
biological clock 45
both/and thinking 85–6, 87
boundaries, age 36–7
Bousfield, L. 84
Bowlby, John 56
Bridges, William 53, 61, 62–5, 68, 89
British Association for Counselling
    and Psychotherapy (BACP) 32, 87
Bronfenbrenner, U. 7
Bytheway, B. 14

capacity to choose 38
career development, counsellors 18,
    28–34
career issues, clients 46
change
    coping with 6–7
    counsellor experience 34
    demographic 45
    evolving life structure 6, 7–9
    perception of 47–8
    structure-changing phases 83, 89, 108
    transtheoretical model 8
    see also transitions
Chaplin, J. 99–100
characters in life stories 73
childist counselling 9
children
    age boundaries 36
    autonomy 38
    capacity to choose 38
    childist counselling 9
    counselling 37–9
    dependency 38–9
    developmental tasks 104
    individuation 51
    power 15–16, 39, 89
    teachable moments 20
    transitions 82
    of young adults 44–5
choice 29–30, 38
clients 16, 34–5, 46, 89–91, 106–7
Cochran, L. 83
Cohler, B.J. 81–3

cohort factors 90
commentaries on Activity Trail 97–113
communication 50, 73, 90
competence 23, 32
concrete learning mode 4
conditional autonomy stage 31
conscious competence 32
consolidating phases 8
conventional stage 31
convoys *see* interpersonal support
    convoys
Cooper, C. 42–3
coping with change 6–7
core narratives 84
counsellors
    age and life stage 16, 90
    autobiographical accounts 33
    clients age and life stage 91
    curriculum vitae Activity Trail
        exercise 10, 28–9, 106
    professional development stages 28–34
    self 31–4
countertransference 50
Crompton, M. 9
Crossley, Michele 112
cultural narratives 83
cultural norms 7
Cumming, E. 20
Cupitt, D. 25
curriculum vitae 28–9, 106

death 48, 55–6, 73, 82–3, 110
death instinct 73
Delworth, U. 30
demographic change 45
dependency
    adolescents 41
    children 38–9
    older adults 49
    of parents 47, 49
desire for love and power 73
developmental...
    psychology 28
    stages 19–26, 103–5
    status of clients 90
    tasks 19–26, 86, 103–5
directiveness 41

Compiled by INDEXING SPECIALISTS (UK) Ltd., 202 Church Road, Hove,
East Sussex BN3 2DJ. Tel: 01273 738299. email: richardr@indexing.co.uk Website:
www.indexing.co.uk